Voice
& Speech
in the Theatre

Voice

& Speech

in the Theatre

FIFTH EDITION

J. CLIFFORD TURNER
edited by Malcolm Morrison

A & C Black • London
Theatre Arts Books / Routledge • New York

2002/13

Fifth edition 2000
A & C Black (Publishers) Limited
35 Bedford Row, London WC1R 4JH

ISBN 0-7136-5193-8

© 2000, 1950, 1956, 1977, 1993, A & C Black (Publishers) Ltd

First published 1950
by Pitman Publishing Ltd
Second edition 1956
Third edition 1977
Fourth Edition 1993

A CIP catalogue record for this book is available from
the British Library.

Published in the USA in 2000 by   /
Theatre Arts Books / Routledge
29 West 35 Street, New York NY10001

ISBN 0-87830-112-7

CIP catalog record available at the Library of Congress.

Cover photograph: © Clive Barda / PAL
Typeset in 11 on 12.5pt Minion
Printed and bound in Great Britain
by Creative Print and Design (Wales), Ebbw Vale

NOTE TO THE FIFTH EDITION

It is somewhat astonishing that this book, which first appeared almost half a century ago, still is relevant and valuable. It has been my pleasure to assist in keeping its format and content current, while remaining faithful to the principles of Clifford Turner. That the basis of the book and the opinions expressed are still vital truths is a tribute to the extraordinary instincts and deep practical knowledge of its author. Not only does he give sound practical advice for the development of a masterful technique; he also injects the sense of an aesthetic concerning acting which is timeless and inspiring.

With this fifth edition I have made a number of adjustments to language, removed references that are no longer relevant and cleared up some few editorial errors which must have been overlooked in the fourth edition. The major change is in response to requests from our readers who asked for more Daily Routines. I have been pleased to include two more complete workouts following Mr. Turner's principles.

I hope that the many who use this book and know it well will approve, and that, as ever, I have helped to perpetuate the life of this immensely practical, sensible and challenging book.

MALCOLM MORRISON

Pray God, your voice, like a piece of uncurrent gold,
be not cracked within the ring.

Hamlet, II, ii

Then they said unto him, Say now Shibboleth; and he said
Sibboleth; for he could not frame to pronounce it right.
Then they took him, and slew him at the passages of Jordan.

Judges, xii, 6

CONTENTS

1 • THE VOICE IN THEORY

When the technical equipment of the actor is considered, voice and speech are of paramount importance. The actor's art, it is true, consists of much more than the delivery of the lines, but take away the element of voice and very little is left. Even if the actor were to forget the aesthetic implications of his or her craft, mere economics compel perfection and care of the voice, and the acquisition of control over speech. It may be retorted that some actors have succeeded in spite of poor or indifferent vocal equipment, and that others have successfully capitalized peculiar individualities of voice and diction. The very highest manifestations of any art are always characterized by a technique so flawless that it is unnoticeable and becomes one with the art itself. This book is not addressed to those whose aim is to exploit their peculiarities. There is a place in the theatre for voices of many types, but no room whatsoever for any voice that is incorrectly managed, or for voice and speech which is not appropriate to the play.

VOICE AND SPEECH AS A HABIT
Voice is instinctive and speech is an acquired habit. The child does not have to learn how to cry and croon, but speech is the result of much laborious experiment, which is forgotten as soon as the movements of the tongue and lips have been repeated a sufficient number of times to set up a habit.

THE RESULTS OF CONDITIONING
Both voice and speech are conditioned by a large number of factors, for example the influence of social and regional environment. No two persons have identical voices, although many have family resemblances, but there are many who make use of identical speech movements.

The actor makes use of the gift of voice and the acquired habit of speech, and some degree of proficiency in the day-to-day use of both has always been obtained before they are employed in the theatre. It is clearly not so with the other arts. In these, the acquisition of a technique is obvious, and the habits that are thereby acquired are conditioned entirely by the art. Voice and speech for the majority are haphazard affairs, but what passes in everyday life will not stand the test of performance in the theatre, and the qualities that are essential for the actor cannot be acquired overnight, let alone during the process of rehearsal. The voice and speech of the embryo actor, then, are already determined before acting begins. Unfortunately, difficulties often arise when bad habits have to be discarded and prejudices overcome before the new habits can be substituted. In many ways it would be simpler for all concerned were he or she in a position to start from scratch.

The text of a play has often most aptly been compared with a musical score. The actor is the link between the dramatist and the audience. The voice is the means by which the dramatist's work is bodied forth, and is the main channel along which thought and feeling are to flow. The voice, in fact, is an instrument, a highly specialized instrument, which is activated and played upon by the actor's intelligence and feeling, both of which have been stimulated by the imaginative power he or she is able to bring to bear upon the dramatist's creation. The actor not only has a most rigorous standard of integrity to which he or she must adhere, but bears a definite responsibility to the dramatist, the director, fellow actors, and the audience.

THE VOICE AS AN INSTRUMENT

Once this is admitted, it is obvious that the most exacting demands are made upon the voice, which is capable of achieving its objectives only when it has become a responsive instrument capable of great refinement of detail. This attitude towards the matter may be likened to the relationship which exists between a musician and the instrument. Supreme moments are achieved only when there is a balance held between the instrument and the person who plays it, and when both contribute equally, for the virtuoso will be hampered by an indifferent instrument, and the tyro will achieve but meagre results from the most sensitive instrument. The two are complementary. And so it is with the actor. Even the most brilliant intellectual and emotional grasp of character and situation will be diminished in effect by poor vocal equipment, and mere voice, whether 'full of sound and fury' or not, will signify next to nothing.

The aim of this book is to indicate the fundamentals of training which will put at the actor's command a technique of voice and speech; a technique which will embody the essentials of the art, but which cannot in the nature of things be in any way final or conclusive.

A technique matures only with the development and maturing of the imagination by which it is controlled and whose servant it is.

THE PRODUCTION OF VOICE

When the term voice is used it refers to the quality of the tone by which a speaker may be identified. But tone pre-supposes a resonator, and a resonator is lifeless and inert until it is activated, and only then are its properties heard. To understand the voice in its essentials, we must understand the importance of a whole sequence of events which must take place before tone results. Before the tone of an instrument such as the violin is heard, the strings must be bowed. The energy of the arm movements is transferred to the strings, which then vibrate, and so set up a note. This note acquires tone through the resonating properties of the wooden belly of the instrument.

Excitor, vibrator, resonator

There are thus three separate and distinct factors to be taken into account—

1. *The Excitor:* the force which is essential to initiate any sound. The energy behind the arm movements of the violinist and the drummer. The breath of the oboe player.
2. *The Vibrator:* that part of the instrument which resists the excitor, or to which the energy of the excitor is transferred. The strings of the violin, the stretched skin of the drum, the reed of the oboe.
3. *The Resonator:* that part of the instrument which amplifies the note resulting from bringing the excitor and vibrator into association. The wooden part beneath the strings of the violin, and the whole of woodwind and brass instruments into which the reed is inserted or into the mouthpiece of which the player blows.

In a violin, as in many other man-made instruments, the tone is determined by the skill of the craftsman who makes the instrument. The instrumentalist, although initially concerned with the setting up of a note which will do nothing to destroy or mar the tone of which the resonator is capable, is primarily concerned with the movements which the particular instrument demands to render the printed score in terms of sound.

VOICE AS A SECONDARY ACTIVITY

The genius of man has enabled him to adapt the function of a number of bodily organs to achieve the same results. This function of the organs is only secondary to their main and vital functions. Thus the air exhaled from the lungs is utilized by man as an excitor. The exhaled air may issue from the lungs as it entered them, as mere breath, or it may be resisted in the larynx by the vocal cords which form the vibrator. The vocal cords work on the principle of a reed, and cause the exhaled air to be cut up into a series of minute puffs which constitute the note. Before this note reaches the outer air it must pass through the pharynx, whose main function is concerned with swallowing. It can then pass through the mouth, one vital function of which is chewing; or the nose, whose main function is associated with respiration and the sensation of smell. These cavities form the triple resonator of the voice. In speakers the tone may be non-existent, may have been impaired through mismanagement of the organs concerned, or may be merely latent. Few speakers utilize the tone of which they are capable, and some employ tone which resembles the sound of their remote ancestors. Others attempt to combine the vital and vocal functions of these cavities, and swallow at the same time as they declaim. Many chew their conversation, while others would seem to attempt the impossible task of smelling the tone as it issues from their noses!

So far no mention has been made of the movable nature of the mouth resonator. This can assume an infinite variety of shapes by reason of the variable position of the tongue and lips, singly or in combination. It is this variation in the shape of the mouth which has the effect of imprinting the character of the vowels on the tone.

QUALITY AND CHARACTER

In listening to a speaker we hear the tone of the voice, which is the result of the effect of the whole resonator upon the note produced. We also hear the character of the sound, due to the change in shape of the resonators. We might, therefore, say that we can recognise who is speaking by the quality, and what they are saying by the characters of the sounds. Clearly it is possible for the quality to be satisfactory and the character unsatisfactory. In other words the tone is good but the pronunciation is bad. In the same way it is possible for the pronunciation to be impeccable, but the tone indifferent. We shall see later that one of the main problems of voice production is to achieve maximum resonation, or tone, for each vowel, without sacrificing the clarity of its character.

CONSONANTS

The resonator possesses the additional function of impeding the free, open passage of the tone and in so doing forms the consonants of a language. Thus the three cavities may be thrown into communication with each other by bringing the lips together and lowering the soft palate, as in the case of M. The mouth may be eliminated as a resonator when the pharynx and nose only are used, as in the case of NG. The resonator may be completely closed and then suddenly opened, as in the case of B. The exit from the mouth may be narrowed in a great variety of ways by bringing the articulatory organs close together as, for example, in V.

Tone and word

The distinction between voice and speech should now be clearer. Voice is tone which is produced by a speaker in a manner exactly analogous to its manner of production in man-made instruments. The words of a printed page, on the other hand, may be regarded as a record of the movements of the speech organs, and correspond to the movement of the instrumentalist when he reads notes from the printed score. When the actor learns his words he is in reality committing to memory the sequence of movements for which the words are the visual symbols.

If this seems a surprising way of regarding the matter, the reader should speak this, or any other sentence which enters the mind, using the breath alone. Do not attempt to read it aloud, or to make the words carry, but speak the words on the breath. There must be no sound in the accepted sense of the word. What you have done could be heard quite easily a short distance away, for you have imprinted the vowel shapes and the articulatory movement on the breath as it issues from the lungs.

When these movements have been recorded they are recalled at the moment of performance. But in order that these movements should reach the members of the audience farthest away from the stage, the excitor, vibrator, and resonator are all brought into service in order to produce tone, on which the movements are superimposed and by means of which the movements are carried to the last rows of the theatre. Every time the actor speaks, this dual character of his instrument is made evident. It is at one and the same time a tone-producing instrument and a word-producing instrument. The human resonator, therefore, excels all others in its complexity and fascination, and yet the resonator, and in fact the whole instrument, behaves perfectly providing its natural functioning is not interfered with, and is developed on correct physiological principles.

BREATH, NOTE, TONE, WORD

This double action of the resonator must be continually borne in mind if the voice is to function correctly: in fact, it is safe to say that when the two functions are confused in training, success is rarely, if ever, achieved. There are, then, four aspects of utterance to be considered in training the voice; namely, the breath, the note, the tone, and the word. Each must be developed on its own merits, in the right order, and related to the rest during this process.

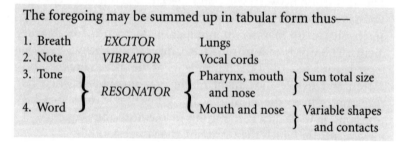

The foregoing may be summed up in tabular form thus—

1. Breath	EXCITOR	Lungs	
2. Note	VIBRATOR	Vocal cords	
3. Tone	} RESONATOR	{ Pharynx, mouth and nose	} Sum total size
4. Word		Mouth and nose	} Variable shapes and contacts

The order of occurrence may now be grasped visually. The breath is seen to be the foundation upon which utterance is built. The first modification of the breath occurs when the vibrating vocal cords cut up the breath stream and in so doing form the note. The whole resonator then modifies the note and imparts tone. The shapes the resonator assumes, and the articulatory movements it makes, modify the tone. Speech, then, is the result of a whole chain of interrelated events. It is heard in perfection only when harmony exists between them, and only then will the instrument respond with subtlety and sensitivity to the intention of the actor.

SPEECH IN THE THEATRE

Speech in the theatre must be governed by the necessity of speaking to large numbers of listeners at one and the same time, so that every word carries convincingly; and yet it must be so controlled that the illusion of reality is not destroyed. Obviously, this is not true of most speech situations, where the demands on the voice are comparatively insignificant. But consider what is demanded of a Juliet in Act III or a Macbeth in Act V. Such roles can never be lightly undertaken, even by the most technically accomplished.

At the opposite extreme we may consider stage dialogue which is written with the express purpose of creating the illusion that what is spoken from the stage is not only true to life but is life itself. In this case the audience is in the position of a privileged spectator for whom the fourth wall of a room has been conveniently removed. It might be argued that such dialogue presents even greater problems for the actor. It is certainly the most deceptive, for the unwary are deceived by its apparent likeness to life, and fall into the trap of adopting the speech habits of real life, under the mistaken impression that these not only serve but also enhance the impression of reality.

All stage dialogue, whether cast in the romantic or in the realistic moulds, is composed, pruned, and shaped to create a designed impression, and Shakespeare, Ibsen, and Noel Coward all demand the same heightened form of utterance, the difference between them being merely one of degree. The two hours' traffic of the stage demands such compression of dialogue that every breath, every note, every tone, and every syllable of every word must be given their due value.

These preliminaries have brought us back to the concept of the voice as an instrument and the script of a play as a musical score which awaits interpretation by the living voice of the actor – created in the actor, and responsive to the emotions engendered by his or her life and art. On this the actor plays by means of articulation, and so brings words to life.

2 • THE VOICE IN PRACTICE

No instrument can be played without making use of the force of the excitor, and we cannot speak at all without using the breath. The way in which we use it is of great importance. Interpretation rests upon the most shaky of foundations if the breath force will not respond automatically to all the demands made upon it by the emotional powers of the artist. Indeed, interpretation cannot even begin until this force is developed and controlled.

CONTROL

It is relatively a simple matter to obtain correctly an increase in the breath supply, but uncontrolled force is a menace to the note and tone of the voice. We need, therefore, not only to obtain sufficient capacity to ensure impeccable phrasing and to bring about all the manifold changes in volume that may be necessary, but also the ability to control the breath so that it is used with the firmness and controlled power that are behind the bow of the violinist.

BREATHING FOR LIFE

It has been noted that the use of the breath as an excitor is secondary to the main and vital function it plays in respiration. It follows, therefore, that the organs concerned must be developed on correct physiological lines. In other words, we are not free to impose a series of movements on our breathing mechanism if these movements are contrary to their natural action, but our minimum requirements must be achieved by developing those movements for which the organs themselves were designed. In breathing exercises, however, the rhythm of the normal breathing cycle is disturbed. In quiet breathing this cycle consists of a comparatively slow intake, a comparatively quick outlet, followed by a pause. In sustained utterance it is obvious that the output takes considerably longer than the intake, and that any pauses which are made are governed by either logical or emotional considerations, and are usually only of momentary duration. In rearranging the timing of these movements in practice, therefore, we are merely preparing ourselves for the conditions which prevail.

BREATHING FOR VOICE

In everyday life breathing is what is termed a reflex act, which means that the movements are carried out without the will being involved. We do not have to say to ourselves that it is some time since a breath was taken so we must breathe again. Nor are we conscious of the movements themselves, except when for some reason they are laboured and in consequence we experience a sense of discomfort. But the essence of a technique is that all movements should be consciously directed until a new habit is formed. Therefore we have to decide which movements of the breathing mechanism will bring about the best results in the voice, and repeat these movements under the direction of the will until they become habitual. They will then automatically come into play whenever the voice is to be used under conditions which make conversational habits unsuitable. Our problem is, firstly, to direct the breathing movements in such a way as to achieve good working capacity, so that the normal functioning of the organs is disturbed to the minimum extent; and, secondly, to regulate and control the exhaled breath, so that the best possible results are achieved when it is used as an excitor to initiate the note. It will be seen later that the method of breathing adopted has most important repercussions on the tone.

THE MECHANISM OF BREATHING

It is common knowledge that the lungs are enclosed in a more or less conical cage formed by the ribs, which increase progressively in size from top to bottom. The base of this cone is formed by the diaphragm, a muscular partition separating the upper and lower parts of the trunk. Air is drawn into the lungs when the size of the chest is increased. This increase may be brought about by the contraction of the muscles which move the ribs and by the descent of the diaphragm when its muscle fibres contract. Not everyone breathes in an identical way and not everyone makes use of both these movements; even when they do, they are not always equally employed. But as they are the movements which must be developed and controlled if a technique is to be established, they must be examined in some detail, so that the extent and nature of the movements, and the manner of adaptation necessary to establish good working capacity and efficient control, may be made clear.

SOME COMMON PROBLEMS

When the muscles which move the ribs contract, they tend to draw the whole cage in an upward and outward direction. The upward pull of the muscles causes them to move outwards as well as upwards, and it is the outward movement of the ribs which should be encouraged. Any tendency to lift the rib cage vertically as a whole must be resisted and there must be no raising of the shoulders. Such movements result in shallow breathing. It is almost impossible to control the breath which is obtained in this manner, for, on speaking, the ribs collapse with inevitable harshness of attack, and control of volume and tone becomes impossible.

BASIC RIB MOVEMENT

Lateral movement is to be encouraged and vertical movement resisted. This lateral expansion of the ribs should be felt at a 'central' level by placing the fingers on the ribs with the thumbs behind, pointing towards the spine, three or four inches above the waist just in front of the armpits. Taking care not to draw the elbows back, direct the ribs to move outwards, sensing the lateral movement as the air is drawn in. The movement should be originated at the point where the thumbs can be felt against the ribs at the back. The sensation should be that the whole of the back widens through from side to side. The wrong sensation is that the ribs and breastbone are thrust forward in front.

This exercise should be the basis of all practice until the sensation is arrived at that the ribs spring out effortlessly to their maximum excursion with no movement whatsoever of the upper part of the rib cage. This will, of course, take time to achieve, although the implication is not that one remains on this exercise until boredom sets in. An important point to note is that the breath should enter and leave the lungs silently. The value of expansion is not increased by the accompaniment of a sustained sniff.

When the correct movement of the ribs has been acquired, the same exercise is performed again, only this time the breath is taken in through the nose and released through the mouth by relaxing the jaw downwards, paying especial attention to the easy unstiffened jaw position and the noiseless emission of the breath. With the jaw in this condition, the breath is then inhaled as well as exhaled silently through the open mouth. The difficulty is increased by counting thus – in, two, three: hold, two, three: out, two, three. The breath must be held without having recourse to tension.

DEVELOPING CONTROL

So far inhalation and exhalation have been of equal duration, but the first step towards control is to hasten the former and to retard the latter, which may be done by employing a shorter count during inhalation and a longer one during exhalation, until eventually the ribs swing out instantaneously but move inwards to a mental count of twenty.

Important note

At this stage, however, no such prolonged exhalation should be attempted. The principal object should be to direct the breath to the right place in the right way. The reader may gradually increase the counting, but never to such an extent that discomfort is experienced. The power to control the outlet of the breath must be acquired gradually, with no attempt to take a short cut.

THE DIAPHRAGM

The diaphragm forms the base of the conical cage, as we have seen. It arches up into the thorax so that it presents a convex surface to the lungs. When it contracts it descends and in so doing tends to displace the organs lying immediately beneath it. These organs are not compressed, however, for the muscles of the upper abdominal wall relax and are moved forwards.

FEELING THE DIAPHRAGM MOVE

This forward movement is most easily observed when one is in a relaxed position lying on the floor. The finger-tips of one hand should be placed just above the waist on the soft part between the ribs. No conscious effort should be made to breathe, and the fingers should merely note, but not assist, the movement. There may, at first, be no movement at all, as the diaphragm is frequently sluggish, and the extent of its downward movement and the ease with which this can be induced varies considerably between one individual and another. The movement of the abdominal wall below the waist should be almost negligible. If there is a decided movement of the whole abdominal wall, the movement is probably being made by these muscles alone, and not as a result of the movement of the

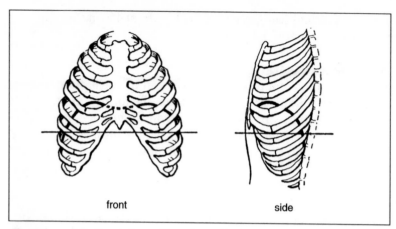

front   side

Fig.1 Ribs and diaphragm in position of rest. The horizontal lines indicate the area to which attention should be drawn when sensing the expansion of the ribs and diaphragm.

diaphragm, and will therefore be incorrect. When the correct movement has been established it should be done in the standing position until it can be performed at will.

DEVELOPING CAPACITY

It should by now be obvious that full capacity should be obtained by combining the movements of the ribs and diaphragm. In this connection there is an important point to note. The diaphragm is attached by its circumference to the lower ribs, so that when these move outwards they draw the edges of the diaphragm with them. The extent of the downward movement of this muscle is thereby restricted. There is, however, no diminution of the breath capacity, since the lack of downward movement is compensated for by the increase in the size of the area in which the diaphragm moves.

It is the equalizing and balancing of the two movements which not only enable us to acquire full capacity but also ensure against an ungainly protrusion of the abdominal wall. It should be noted that men and women often differ to a considerable extent in the ratio of the two movements. Women, on the whole, tend to use the diaphragm too little and to rely too exclusively on rib movement, whilst many men use the ribs insufficiently and rely almost exclusively on the downward movement of the diaphragm. To attempt to gain capacity in either of these ways is to court trouble.

BASIC RIB AND DIAPHRAGM MOVEMENT

The fingers of one hand should now be placed on the ribs as described and the finger-tips of the other hand in the region where the result of the diaphragm movement may be felt. On a mental count of one direct the ribs to move outwards. On two, the diaphragm is to descend: the hand at the centre is moved forward. On three, the lungs are deflated and both hands move inwards in following the movement of the chest walls. The counting should be rhythmical and slow, and the movements should be regular and definite and should occupy the whole of the time taken by the mental count. Short staccato movements are not to be used. Care must again be taken to check any tendency to raise the ribs and shoulders and the whole movement must be easy and comfortable. If there is any feeling of strain or discomfort, it will probably mean that the movements are being performed too vigorously, so that an unmanageable quantity of breath is being taken in.

In cultivating deep breathing, it must be remembered we are developing the bellows of the instrument and that the normal breathing cycle is being disturbed. In other words, we are taking in more breath than the body actually requires. Slow, regular practice will be the most successful in the long run and will result in full capacity with an absence of discomfort. It is pointless to attempt to force the pace.

DEVELOPMENT OF BREATH CONTROL

The breath thus obtained must be conserved by controlling its outlet, not only so that all the demands of phrasing may be met, but also that the note of the voice may be initiated with correct pressure and attack. Uncontrolled force is undesirable in playing any instrument. What success would the violinist have if the force necessary to set the strings in vibration were not applied under control? A similar question could equally be asked of the pianist and the singer. Innumerable speakers try to get by when they are deficient in control, and then wonder why they do not get the best results.

Control, in the first instance, means delaying the rate of exhalation. This can be achieved by using separately the two movements already described. Thus, a full breath is taken by the simultaneous movements of the ribs and diaphragm. The breath is then emitted by means of the rising diaphragm alone. The ribs are then allowed to descend. This should be done to a count of three. The two exercises may be set out thus –

A '*One.*'   The ribs are expanded. Hand is moved outwards.
     '*Two.*'   The diaphragm is lowered. Hand is moved forward.
     '*Three.*'   The ribs descend and the diaphragm is raised simultaneously, thus deflating the lungs. Both hands move inwards in following the movement.

B '*One.*'   The ribs are expanded and the diaphragm is lowered simultaneously, thus obtaining full capacity. Fingers of both hands are moved outwards.
     '*Two.*'   The diaphragm is raised. Fingers of hand at centre move inwards. Ribs out, resting against the fingers.
     '*Three.*'   The ribs are lowered. Fingers of other hand move inwards.

The object of separating the movements in the first exercise is chiefly to ensure full rib movement before the diaphragm descends, but the separation in itself is a valuable exercise in control for those in whom the combined movement is already habitual. Ribs and diaphragm ultimately always move together as in the first count of the second exercise. The difficulty of both exercises is increased by prolonging the time taken over exhalation. In the first exercise the two movements grouped under 'Three' could eventually be performed to a count of twenty. In the second exercise the movements under 'Two' and 'Three' should be performed to a count of ten each. Eventually! Do not jeopardize the final result by forcing the pace.

When the second of the above exercises can be done easily, we are ready to pass to the final form of control which is really an extension of what has already been achieved. For this the movements are exactly the same as for the second exercise, but the movement under 'Three' is omitted. Thus, with the hands in position, a full breath is taken. Breath is then exhaled by raising the diaphragm, but when this has taken place the ribs are not allowed to descend but remain extended. The diaphragm is then contracted to replenish the breath supply, and again is allowed to rise to expel a quantity of breath. Breath is alternately inhaled and exhaled by the diaphragm which contracts and relaxes rhythmically. The fingers of one hand sense this movement, but the fingers on the ribs sense that there is no inward movement of the chest walls. This is sometimes found to be difficult but, with perseverance, ultimately becomes as simple and easy as breathing in any other way.

RIB-RESERVE BREATHING

This method of control has been aptly termed rib-reserve breathing,* for the maintained elevation of the ribs holds back a reserve of air which we may utilize whenever there is a special need. No speaker who develops rib-reserve is ever in the position of speaking on the tail end of the breath, so that audibility, as far as the breath is responsible, is ensured. Support is given to the note, so that steady, even pitch is easily maintained and the danger of vibrato diminished. It is a powerful aid in tone building, although discussion of this aspect of rib-reserve must be deferred until Chapter 3. The best possible way to develop rib-reserve is to use it whilst walking. That the ribs are expanded may be sensed by the tighter fit of one's clothes. The movements of the diaphragm are timed to the movement of the limbs, and the number of breaths taken by the diaphragm to each step may gradually be decreased. The arms, legs, and possibly the head, are moving, so there is little likelihood of muscular tension arising, which is always a possibility when attention is drawn to a movement of which we are not normally conscious.

MAINTAINING THE RESERVE

In the course of time it is found quite easy to maintain the ribs in the expanded position during the sustained utterance of a passage of some length. This is possible owing to the relationship which exists between the diaphragm and the abdominal muscles. These are what are known as antagonistic muscles, which means that when one contracts the other relaxes and vice versa. This action of muscles can very easily be observed by grasping the arm and noting what occurs when the arm is alternately extended and bent. If the muscles responsible for these movements contract simultaneously, the arm is stiffened and rigidity sets in. Movement again becomes possible only when one muscle relaxes and gives way to the opposi-

---

* For the use of the term 'rib-reserve,' and for many of the views expressed in the following pages, I am indebted to the late W. A. Aikin, M.D., whose pupil I was at one time privileged to be.

tion exerted by the contracting muscle. Much the same conditions apply where the diaphragm and abdominal muscles are concerned. In inhalation, the diaphragm is active and contracts and the abdominal muscles yield by relaxing; but in breathing out, the diaphragm is passive, and will return to its arched position only at the rate at which the abdominal muscles contract. These may be brought under the direct control of the will, and so the rate at which the breath passes out of the lungs can be determined.

It is by the use of rib-reserve that we gain firm and sensitive control over the force of the breath. Failure to achieve this control results in uncontrolled force, which will do nothing but hamper the development of tone.

RELAXATION

Side by side with the development of breath control it is necessary to cultivate the ability to relax. Nothing is so destructive of one's ease of tone as the tensing of those muscles which are not essential for the performance of a specific movement. Extreme cases of tension lead to loss of voice and often to permanent impairment of the vocal cords. It is well, therefore, to develop the power to relax at will from the outset, as this is just as essential to good voice as the performance of a series of graded exercises. All the exercises in the world will not lead to success if tension is present.

Speech is movement. The movement of the respiratory organs has been described. Before this breath is heard as speech it is modified in innumerable ways by the movement of certain organs brought about by muscular contraction and relaxation. In speaking the foregoing sentence well over forty muscles are involved. Other things being equal, perfection of utterance is achieved only when perfection of muscular co-ordination is reached, and such co-ordination is impossible if the action of these muscles is hampered by tension.

THE EFFECTS OF TENSION

The conditions under which an actor practises his or her art are peculiarly conducive to tension. It is a paradox that technique is the means by which outward and inward causes of nervous tension may be circumvented, and that perfection of technique never results before the ability to eliminate tension has been acquired. Technique enables the imagination to flower. Tension causes it to wither at the roots so that nothing but a pale replica of the intention is revealed. In his book *My Life in Art*, Stanislavski describes how an actor so schooled himself that the muscular tensions to which he was prone disappeared the moment he made his entrance on to the stage. Again, in *An Actor Prepares* he recalls how a certain actress of unusual temperament was able to free her emotion only on rare occasions. At other times she had recourse to effort. At dramatic moments unintentional facial contractions would creep in. Eventually this was overcome with an accompanying relaxation of the other muscles of her body and a consequent freeing of her emotional powers. These two cases illustrate the importance of becoming aware of the relation between the mind and the body so that relaxation can be induced at will, even when conditions tend to produce the opposite effect. In the case of the actress, the facial effort was communicated to other parts of the body, possibly to the voice, with consequent diminution of effectiveness.

EXERCISES FOR RELAXATION

Relaxation, when it has been induced, assists one to cope with the situation. One feels better when relaxed and, consequently, one is less inclined to worry. From the strictly vocal angle, the relaxation of the large muscles controlling posture must first be achieved so that a sense of ease pervades the whole body in order to induce relaxation in the smaller but no less vital muscles concerned in voice.

The best position in which to bring about an awareness of relaxation is to lie on the floor or some other flat surface which will not yield to the weight of the body. The back of the head should be supported by a cushion or a fairly thick book. The arms should lie at the sides with the palms of the hands downwards and the elbows roughly six inches out from the sides. With the heels some eighteen inches apart, the legs and feet should be allowed to rotate outwards under their own weight. The knees should then be drawn up towards the ceiling until the feet rest flat on the floor with no sensation of tightness across the instep.

In this position the spine should be allowed to mould itself, as it were, along its whole length to the surface of the floor, but should not be forced down in any way. It should not be possible to insert the fingers between the floor and the spine. If the fingers can be inserted, draw the knees up towards the chin until the feet are off the floor with the thighs parallel to the chest. Concentrating on the position of the spine, allow the legs to resume their former position, disturbing the back as little as possible.

The body is now inert, the muscles which hold the body erect being flaccid. All activity should be taken out of the limbs, so that if someone were to lift the limbs, no muscle tension or spasm would occur. The mind, however, should actively be recording the ease resulting from such deep relaxation so that the sensation may be recalled at will. In addition, the head and shoulders should be mentally directed outwards from the body.

When lying relaxed in this way, the body is in an ideal position in which to observe and check the movement of the diaphragm. To do this, transfer the hands to the abdominal wall immediately above the waist and, without breathing consciously, note the outward and inward movement of the abdominal wall as the diaphragm respectively contracts and relaxes.

Before standing, allow the legs to extend until they assume the position first described. While doing this the attention should be concentrated on the spine so that its position is disturbed as little as possible. On standing, first recall the sensation of ease experienced in the supine position, and, while maintaining this condition, direct the ribs outward and breathe by making small panting movements with the diaphragm. The movement in and out should be regular and equal and, as proficiency is gained, should take place extremely rapidly. This is a purely technical exercise, valuable in that it establishes independence of diaphragm movement and is a means of developing the power of holding the breath and keeping the throat open at the same time. The breath may be taken through the nose or the mouth.

Logically, these remarks on relaxation should have preceded those on breathing. The voice is a living instrument and as much a part of the body as any other organ. It will not function at its best unless we develop it in relation to the body as a whole. Perfect breathing will never be achieved if the body is not relaxed and posture, in consequence, is bad with the body out of true alignment. When posture is good, however, it helps in the acquisition of rib-reserve, which comes to be sensed as part of the general bodily attitude towards movement as a whole, and not only as the most effective form of breathing to obtain the best results from the voice.

APPLICATION OF THE EXERCISES

Assuming the exercises so far given can be carried out, it remains to bridge the gap between breathing as a technical exercise and as a practical means of getting the best results from the voice. The transition should be made gradually, as the attempt to sustain a long speech with the aid of rib-reserve is generally found diffficult. The necessary slow, firm, upward movement of the diaphragm may be brought about by a simple exercise.

Exercise 1

Count up to ten or twelve whilst maintaining the ribs in the raised position. The backs of the fingers of one hand should be placed where the movement of the diaphragm may be sensed. With firm even pressure breathe out whilst counting aloud: one (breathe in); one, two (breathe in); one, two, three (breathe in), and so on up to twelve. The diffficulty may be increased by varying the volume of tone used.

Exercise 2

Proceeding exactly as before, start the counting with full, resonant tone, and, as the counting proceeds, decrease the volume, still maintaining good tone. Reverse the procedure by starting the count clearly, but extremely quietly, and, maintaining good tone throughout, gradually increase the pressure, and consequently the volume, ending the count on a full, powerful tone which, however, does not suggest shouting.

Exercise 3

To speak a sonnet whilst using rib-reserve breathing is to provide oneself with a simple, yet searching test of one's attainments in breathing. The sonnet should preferably be one in which each line is more or less self-contained in thought and the mood is expressed objectively. Drayton's *The Parting*, Shakespeare's *When in the chronicle of wasted time*, and Andrew Lang's *The Odyssey* are random examples. In the first, where the phrasing is relatively simple, the breath pause coincides with the end of each line, which means that a fresh diaphragm breath is taken for each line and that the ribs do not descend until the last word has been spoken. In all three the tone must receive firm, even support right through from the first word to the last.

Exercise 4

Breathe in and, at the same time, raise the arms at the sides to shoulder level. Bend the arms at the elbows and rest the fingers on the nape of the neck. With the arms in this position and with the shoulders well down, breathe in and out, whilst keeping the ribs extended. In this position speak the following–

> Two households, both alike in dignity,
> In fair Verona, where we lay our scene,
> From ancient grudge break to new mutiny,
> Where civil blood makes civil hands unclean.
> From forth the fatal loins of these two foes
> A pair of star-crost lovers take their life;
> Whose misadventured piteous overthrows
> Do with their death bury their parents' strife.
> The fearful passage of their death-mark'd love,
> And the continuance of their parents rage,
> Which, but their children's end, naught could remove,
> Is now the two hours' traffic of our stage;
> The which if you with patient ears attend,
> What here shall miss, our toil shall strive to mend.
>   (*Romeo and Juliet*, Prologue.)

Your attention throughout this section has been directed to one of the focal points of the speech mechanism, and to the basic area of control, and from now on whenever breathing is referred to the use of rib-reserve will be implied.

It has been impossible to indicate the length of time it takes to acquire this form of breathing, as it will vary from individual to individual. It is much better to take things gradually and to master each exercise before passing to the next, than to attempt them one after the other in rapid succession. In any case, such a procedure would probably end in failure. Little by little is good advice where breathing is concerned, but be sure it is little and frequent.

The foregoing exercises may be summarized thus–

1. General exercise on relaxation.
2. Free, easy rhythmic expansion of lower ribs at the 'central' level.
3. Expansion of ribs, followed by descent of diaphragm, followed by exhalation to a rhythmic count.
4. Simultaneous expansion of ribs and diaphragm. Breath exhaled, first by means of raising diaphragm, followed by descent of ribs.
5. As above; only ribs are maintained in their expanded position, which is felt to be part of the poised attitude of the body towards the voice as a whole.
6. Maintaining the expanded rib position, breathe by making small panting movements with the diaphragm.
7. Speak a passage of moderate length whilst maintaining the raised ribs. This may be assisted in the first place by placing the hands behind the head as described.

OTHER ADVANTAGES OF RIB-RESERVE

In conclusion, mention must be made of several secondary advantages of rib-reserve. It is silent, always providing that tension in the airways is not present. Nothing is more ridiculous than when vigorous delivery is punctuated by a series of snorts or gasps as the breath enters the lungs: a point to be borne in mind when rapidity exercises are introduced. It is invisible. Delivery is equally ridiculous when punctuated by a series of heaves and shoulder raisings.

Any material will furnish opportunities for developing breath control, but as the demands made upon the breath are brought home most by rhetorical speeches, the following are suggested for further study–

> *Troilus and Cressida*, opening chorus.
> *Henry VIII*, opening chorus.
> *Henry V*, any of the choruses.
> *Henry IV*, ii, the epilogue.
> *As You Like It*, the epilogue.

3 · THE TONE

So far, the breath has been treated as if it had an existence apart from the other factors of note, tone, and word. Although, as we have seen, this is not so, it is best in the first instance to regard the breath in this light, since success in managing the remaining factors depends upon the correct exploitation of the force of the breath.

It would seem that the next logical step to take would be to develop the note, as the first modification of the breath takes place in the larynx where the note itself is formed. There are, however, a number of reasons for by-passing the note at this stage, the most important of which will be discussed later (p. 48). The point to be made here is that before the note reaches our ears it too must of necessity undergo a modification, as the resonator through which the note must pass is between the vocal cords and the outer air. On its outward passage, therefore, the note gains tone, good, bad, or indifferent, through the property of resonation.

TRAINING THE RESONATOR

The resonator, then, comes next in order of training, so that we may develop its powers and control its use, and thus make its influence on the note as perfect as possible. Take the resonator away from the strings of an instrument and what is left to the executant? He can play the notes, but the sound of the strings minus the tone of the instrument would be reminiscent of the tinklings of a hurdy-gurdy. The actor who fails to develop tone is in the same predicament. He has nothing on which to play but the comparatively feeble notes of a reed. He too could vary the notes, and also carry out articulatory movement, but the resultant sound would be meagre and of a papery texture, reminiscent of the sixth age that lies ahead –

> . . . his big manly voice,
> Turning again toward childish treble, pipes
> And whistles in his sound.
>
> (*As You Like It*, II. vii.)

GOOD TONE

The tone of the actor's voice must be flexible and responsive to a high degree. The intention clearly must not be to reduce acting to the terms of vocal technique, however good this may be, although cases could be cited in which this has unfortunately occurred; but the bulk of the actor's work will, in all probability, call for generous and full tone and all his work will call for forwardness of production, unless character or situation demands a modification.

THE PRINCIPAL RESONATORS

The resonator of the voice consists of the three principal cavities above the larynx. These are the pharynx, the mouth, and the nose. The pharynx is a tubular cavity, the walls of which are muscular. The mouth is, roughly, hemispherical in shape. The cheeks form the walls, and the lips and jaw a variable orifice or outlet for the tone. The tongue forms the floor of this resonator and the roof consists of the hard palate, immediately behind the upper teeth, and its continuation, the soft palate, which terminates in the uvula. The soft palate is freely movable and may be raised or lowered by muscular action. This valve-like action of the soft palate opens or closes the entrance to the third resonator, the nose. This is a more or less triangular cavity largely occupied by bony structures.

The size and shape of these cavities determine to a very large extent what we hear, and give rise to general and particular resonation. It is essential that the difference between the two should be grasped, and to this end some aspects of tone already touched upon must be elaborated.

VOICE QUALITY

What general resonation means may best be understood by analogy. If notes of identical pitch and volume were to be played on the violin and piano one after the other, no one would be likely to mistake them, even although the instruments themselves were unseen. The two notes would be similar and dissimilar. The elements of pitch and volume would be identical. We account for the difference we should hear by saying that the two sounds differ in quality. Voices differ from each other in the same way. Two persons who possess identical *AH* vowel sounds could speak or sing them at the same pitch and with the same volume. We should be able to distinguish between the two voices because the general quality of the voices would be different. It is, for example, general quality which enables us to recognize voices over the telephone before the speaker's name is revealed. Various adjectives are brought into service to express the effect made on our senses by voices of different quality. We speak of the tone of voices as bright or dull, rich or thin, hard or soft, pleasing or raucous, irritating, maddening, and doubtless other epithets will occur to the reader! Other things being equal, it is the size and shape of the cavities which are responsible for the differences. Size and shape are the inner features of the instrument, so to speak, and just as no two faces are exactly alike, no two persons possess identical inner features. One may have a highly arched palate or a long neck. One may have small lips and another a large nose!

BALANCED TONE

We may say that the tone is at its best when each section of the resonator contributes more or less equally to produce the sum total effect. Excessive use of the mouth and too little use of the pharynx will result in thin, reedy tone. Excessive use of the pharynx results in heavy, dull tone. Excessive use of the nose results in an overdose of nasality. In some cases complete absence of nasal resonance results in a tight, whining twang. In developing the tone, therefore, we shall not achieve our goal unless we acquire the power of controlling the quota of resonance that each cavity contributes to make up the overall impression.

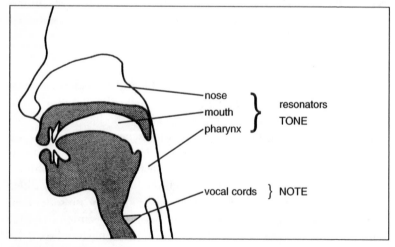

Fig.2 The resonators of the voice.

Each of the three resonators possesses an inherent size and shape, and these inner features determine the general quality or tone. We think of full, resonant sonorous tone as being the result of well-expanded resonators, and of thin, reedy tone as the result of the opposite conditions. This aspect of the tone, then, is referable to the size of the cavities.

THE VOWELS

Not only does the resonator possess this inherent size and shape, but one section of it, the mouth, by reason of the movable tongue, lips and jaw, has the power of assuming a great diversity of shapes. It is our ability to alter the shape of the mouth which enables us to impress the character of the vowels on the tone.

> The *general quality or tone* may be heard as a constant factor owing to the constant *size*, and more or less constant general configuration, of the resonator, while, at the same time, the *specific resonance* changes according to the vowel *shape* through which the note passes. We see that every vowel is a musical note which is the result of the operation of the exciter, the vibrator, and the resonator, and that the latter not only possesses the function of imparting tone, but also that of determining the character of the vowel by reason of the shape through which the tone is moulded.

We cannot materially alter the inherent shape of the cavities. If the palate is highly arched, for example, it cannot be altered, and if the mouth is large it cannot be reduced. A great deal can, and usually must, be done, however, with the contribution each cavity makes towards the total effect.

EXPANDING THE RESONATOR

In expanding the resonator it is of advantage to start with the position in which it is normally the most open, the position of the vowel sound *AH*. For this, the teeth should be approximately one inch apart. The lips must lie loosely on the teeth and play no active part in assuming the position. It is especially important that their corners should not be drawn back. The tongue should lie flat on the floor of the mouth with its tip touching the inner surface of the lower front teeth. The soft palate should be raised. There must be a sense of openness and freedom through absence of constricting tension.

The open jaw and the forward tongue for *AH* opens the resonator at two vital regions where narrowing and constriction most often occur, namely, at the jaw and at the junction of the mouth and throat. It is simple to open the jaw for this vowel, but not so simple to open it for all vowels, and more diffficult to maintain the open position in speaking. It is not easy to open the throat, and yet it is essential to do so if throaty tone is to be avoided.

The resonator may be expanded still further by means of rib-reserve breathing, which has the effect of drawing down the larynx from below, thus bringing about an increase in the size of the pharynx. The physiological explanation of how this comes about need not concern us here. That this does occur can be demonstrated, and the beneficial effects of the expansion of the lower resonator are heard as practice develops. But the enlargement of this cavity can only be brought about indirectly by means of correct poise, controlled breathing, and an absence of tension throughout the resonator. Any attempt consciously to bring about this enlargement is doomed to failure, and will successfully bring about those conditions of tension which it is essential to avoid.

ACHIEVING GOOD TONE

There are three regions or areas of expansion. Of these only one can be seen and felt. We can see and feel the open jaw, and the tongue tip makes known its whereabouts through its highly developed sense of touch. The open throat can be observed to some extent through the use of a mirror, but we can feel it is open only in a very minor degree. We need to develop and train our sense of hearing so that by its acuity and awareness we may bring about the right degree of openness in this area. We can neither see nor feel the extent to which the pharynx is expanded and must rely entirely on the evidence of our ears. In developing tone, therefore, two of our senses enter as controlling factors: touch and hearing. By means of the former we sense that the jaw is open and the tongue is forward, and that the lips are doing what is required of them. Through the sense of movement in our respiratory organs we may check the breathing and make sure that by keeping the ribs expanded we are assisting pharyngeal expansion. It is in this way that the resonator is enlarged at its two extremities, and through the openness of the whole cavity we achieve tone with full-throated ease.

WHISPERING

The by-passing of the note, to which reference has already been made, is not only theoretical but also practical. In examining the properties of the resonators we are best able to understand their ultimate effect on the note if this is temporarily eliminated. By so doing we learn to understand the action of the cavities, and also develop the resonator on its own merits, and so bring about all the conditions which are favourable to effective resonation.

The other reason for proceeding in this manner is that by breathing or whispering through the cavities we acquire the power of eliminating any tendency to constrict the passages, which would have the effect of diminishing their size and would result in defective resonation. The breath to be used for such purposes is a pure whisper as distinct from any forced or stage whisper. No effort must be made to make the breath carry to any great distance, and the breath must not be prefixed by any clicking sound. If the breath be thought of as an *H* sound, there is little likelihood of this occurring.

In training the resonator our initial aims are—
1. Expansion of the cavities in order to impart full sonority to the note.
2. The achievement of balanced resonation, so that no one cavity predominates to the detriment of the total effect.
3. Perfection of the shapes which mould the tone and give it particular character in the form of vowels.

RESONANT PITCH

If we breathe out with the resonator in the position for the vowel AH, as defined, we at first hear nothing more than the character of the vowel. On listening carefully, however, we hear that this vowel possesses a note of a definite and distinctive pitch which is the result of breathing out through the resonating cavities in this position and in this only. This pitch is referred to as the whispered or resonant pitch, as distinct from the vocal pitch which is present only when the vocal cords are in action. We cannot vary the resonant pitch to any great extent without altering the character of the vowel, but the character of the vowel may remain constant while the pitch of the vocal note may be varied considerably as in singing. The resonant pitch is heard more distinctly if the breath is directed to the ear by holding one hand a few inches in front of the mouth and the other close to, but not touching, the ear.

> The resonant pitch is fixed and determined by the size of the resonator, which obeys the laws governing the action of all cavities. The pitch of a large resonator is lower than the pitch of a small resonator. The pitch of a resonator is also determined by the number and size of its openings. In a resonator with one opening the pitch is lowered if this opening is diminished in size and raised if it is increased.

VARIATIONS IN RESONANT PITCH

Now the whispered pitch of *AH* will vary very slightly in individual cases, primarily because we do not all possess resonators of identical size, and it may at first be found that the whispered pitch the reader succeeds in obtaining will not match that which is given in these pages. This is due to the fact that the positions here described represent positions of maximum resonation which are obtainable only after training has begun. At this stage, however, the principles are more important than the actual pitches recorded. During training, there is invariably some lowering of the resonant note with consequent enrichment of resonation when the vocal note is introduced. For a man a good average resonant note for *AH* is C on the treble clef, and for a woman E flat on the treble clef.

MAINTAINING TONE

The position for the vowel *AH*, as defined, is favourable to the maximum expansion of the cavities. It is of little use, however, to have one vowel on which satisfactory resonance may be obtained, and yet this is precisely the position in which the majority of untrained speakers find themselves. With such speakers, in passing from *AH* to *EE*, for example, the jaw is immediately closed and the lips are widened almost to the position for a grin. Thus, in forming the series of vowels which fall between these two positions, the tone deteriorates as the successive stages of jaw-closing and lip-spreading are assumed.

In order to prevent such deterioration of tone, we must train ourselves to move the tongue and, for other vowels, the lips, irrespectively of the jaw. Vowels, as we have seen, are the result of altering the shape of the resonator by these means. If, therefore, we acquire the ability to assume the correct shapes without altering the size of the resonator, we shall reach a state in which the tone will be present as a constant factor while the specific character varies with the changing shapes. It is in this way that a 'line' of resonance is achieved which in its turn makes the use of sustained tone possible, and this is one of the distinguishing features of the well-managed voice.

AH – THE BEGINNING POSITION
This can be best obtained by thinking of certain aspects of the *AH* position as basic positions for all vowels, which are differentiated from *AH* merely by rounding the lips or raising the tongue. The forward tongue tip and the controlled breathing are constant factors, therefore; the lip rounding and the tongue raising are variable factors and are determined by the particular vowel to be spoken or sung. There are, usually, small changes in jaw position to obtain the various vowel sounds. Although it is desirable to minimize this jaw movement in order to obtain maximum resonance, care should be taken not to develop rigidity and tension in the jaw.

Exercise 1
Maintaining the jaw in its open position the lips should now be rounded to the size of a pencil. On breathing out we recognize the character of the vowel *OO*, but in reducing the size of the opening we hear that the resonant pitch has, in consequence, fallen by an interval of a fifth. These two positions should be alternated until the lip movement for *OO* can be performed –

HAH, H́OO. HAH, H́OO. HAH, H́OO. HAH, H́OO. HAH, H́OO.

Exercise 2
Starting from the basic *AH* position, and making sure the tongue tip is against the lower teeth, the body of the tongue should be raised high up in front of the mouth. It is especially important to resist the tendency of the lips to assume a spread position. They should remain as for *AH*. On breathing out, we hear the character of the vowel *EE*, but in raising the tongue we have diminished the size of the mouth and notice that in consequence the pitch has risen by an interval of an octave. These two positions should be alternated until the tongue movement can be made independently of the jaw and lips –

HAH, H́EE. HAH, H́EE. HAH, H́EE. HAH, H́EE. HAH, H́EE.

SOME THINGS TO WATCH FOR

1. Some difficulty is usually experienced in assuming these positions independently of the jaw, and this is especially the case when the tongue is raised. The use of a mirror is of help, and it is valuable to place the fingers of one hand on the chin as an aid in checking the tendency of the lower jaw to move upwards.

2. Many find it extremely difficult to prevent the lips from spreading in passing from *AH* to *EE* when the steady jaw position has been arrived at. In addition to watching the change of shape, the tendency to widen the opening may be resisted if each forefinger is placed at the sides of the lips when the *AH* position is taken up. The fingers do not prevent the widening by exerting pressure, but assist the lips to remain relaxed during the change of shape by a consciousness of the absence of movement through the sense of touch. The position of the resonator should be present to the mind, rather than the vowel which the shape produces. It has been remarked that all speakers habitually widen the lips for a whole series of vowels. If in practising, therefore, we think of the vowel itself, naturally the lips will only too readily repeat the old, bad, habitual movement.

MORE EXERCISES TO DEVELOP RESONANT PITCH

With precautions taken not to spread the lips or close the jaw, the succeeding exercises should be carried out rhythmically and stressed as indicated. One starts or returns to the open, relaxed *AH* position, altering only the position of the tongue or lips as required. When the ability to direct the movements has been acquired, the exercise should be linked with breathing as indicated on the following page.

HAH H́OO, HAH H́EE, HAH H́OO, HAH H́EE, HAH H́OO, HAH H́EE, HAH H́OO, HAH H́EE.

HAH H́EE, HAH H́OO, HAH H́EE, HAH H́OO, HAH H́EE, HAH H́OO, HAH H́EE, HAH H́OO.

HAH H́EE HAH H́OO, HAH H́OO HAH H́EE, HAH H́EE HAH H́OO, HAH H́OO HAH H́EE.

HEE HAH HOO, HEE HAH HOO, HEE HAH HOO, HEE HAH HOO, HEE HAH HOO HEE.

HOO HAH HEE, HOO HAH HEE, HOO HAH HEE, HOO HAH HEE, HOO HAH HEE HOO.

HAH HOO HAH HEE, HAH HOO HAH HEE, HAH HOO HAH HEE, HAH HOO HAH HEE.

HOO HEE HOO HEE HOO HEE HOO HEE HOO HEE HOO HEE HOO HEE HOO HEE.

It is essential that each exercise should be performed rhythmically. In the course of time it will be noticed that in each case a jingle of notes is heard. The clearer and more defined this jingle is made, the better for the clarity of the vowels. The rapidity of the exercises is gradually increased whenever the movements can be correctly executed. Each exercise becomes doubly effective as the agility of the lips and tongue is developed in moving accurately, and with rapidity, from one position to another, whilst maintaining the basic conditions conducive to good tone.

TONE AND BREATH CONTROL
It is but one step farther to control the breathing at the same time as the movements are being carried out. The position for rib-reserve is assumed, and the ribs remain extended whilst the breath passes out and in by the raising and lowering of the diaphragm. When this can be done satisfactorily, a separate breath is used for each position, whilst the ribs remain extended. Thus the diaphragm performs small panting movements, and each position is made audible on the outgoing breath alone. This exercise constitutes a simple and yet valuable training in co-ordination of the two sets of movements. It is a fairly big step to pass to this exercise, and it is usually necessary to develop the panting exercise as suggested on page 18 before it is brought into association with the changing vowel shapes.

MORE VOWELS WITH LIP ROUNDING
Both *OO* and *EE* represent extreme positions of the tongue and lips respectively. Between *OO* and *AH*, four intermediate degrees of lip rounding give rise to the vowels in 'could, code, cawed, cod,' repre-

sented by the symbols *oo, OH, AW, ŏ*. For *OH*, the lips are rounded approximately to thumb size. For AW, they are rounded approximately to the size of the first and third fingers with the second placed on top of them. Intermediate roundings between *OO* and *OH* and *AW* and *AH* give rise to *o͞o* and *ŏ*. But such indications are merely rough and ready and will not necessarily result in the vowels which it is my intention to indicate. A much better guide to their formation is to be found in their whispered pitches. In passing through this series from *OO* to *AH*, we successively increase the size of the opening and, as we have seen, the effect of thus increasing the size of the opening of a resonator will be to raise its resonant note. In whispering this series, therefore, the following scale of notes may be heard.

Average Man

Whispered vowel					
OO	o͞o	OH	AW	ŏ	AH
Cooed	could	code	cawed	cod	card

Average Woman

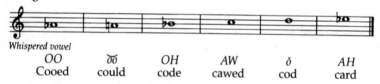

Whispered vowel					
OO	o͞o	OH	AW	ŏ	AH
Cooed	could	code	cawed	cod	card

MORE VOWELS WITH TONGUE RAISING

In between *AH* and *EE*, six degrees of tongue raising produce the shapes for vowels in '*hut, hurt, hat, head, hate, hit.*' In this series the lips are not involved and should remain in the position they assume for *AH*, that is, the opening of the resonator is of a constant size. But the tongue in moving forwards and upwards successively diminishes the size of the mouth as a resonator, and thus produces a rising scale of whispered resonances for these vowels.

Average Man

Whispered vowel							
AH	ŭ	ER	ă	ĕ	AY	ĭ	EE
hard	hut	hurt	hat	head	hate	hit	heat

Average Woman

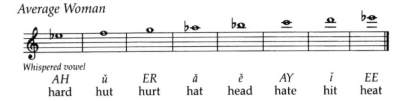

Whispered vowel

AH	ŭ	ER	ă	ě	AY	ĭ	EE
hard	hut	hurt	hat	head	hate	hit	heat

THE RESONATOR SCALE

There is an important difference between the two series. Every time we breathe out through any vowel shape, the breath passes through two cavities, each of which must of necessity possess its own resonant pitch, as each must be of a certain size. In the series *AH* to *EE*, every time the body of the tongue moves forwards and upwards, it diminishes the size of the mouth, as we have seen. Every forward and upward movement, however, must increase the size of the pharynx, as the sum total size of the two cavities together is constant. In this series, therefore, we hear a double scale of notes rising in the mouth and falling in the neck.

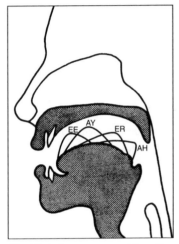

Fig. 3 Relative tongue positions for EE, AY, ER and AH.

In the series *AH* to *OO* there is no such disparity between the relative size of the two cavities, which to all intents and purposes are in unison. The whole scale when set out appears –

Scale of whispered resonances
Average Man

Whispered vowel

OO o͞o OH AW ŏ AH ŭ ER ă ě AY ĭ EE

Average Woman

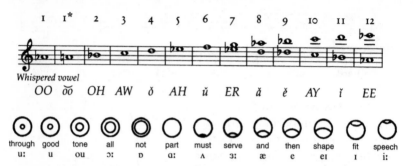

The vowels are numbered for convenience and to prevent ambiguous reference. The circle beneath each vowel denotes the open, expanded condition of the resonator and the open jaw which do not change throughout the whole scale. The inner circle, from 1 to 4, denotes the gradual increase in the size of the lip opening; and the segments, from 6 to 12, the gradual decrease in the size of the mouth consequent upon the raising of the tongue. The phonetic symbols, underneath the keywords, are included here and elsewhere in this book for those who are phonetically minded. They should be ignored by those to whom they are unfamiliar.

There is often some difficulty in hearing the lower resonant notes of the vowels after *AH*, as it is, at first, difficult to dissociate the pitch of the vowels from their character. They may be more easily distinguished by cupping the hands over the ears and listening from within. These lower resonant notes are made very audible and distinct by placing one finger on the base of the lower resonator, just above the larynx, and tapping it with a pencil for each position the tongue assumes.

SIMPLE AND COMPOUND VOWELS

Each of these vowels demands an unchanging position of the resonator, and on this account they may be termed simple vowels, as distinct from compound vowels which demand more than one position. *OH* and *AY* are two exceptions, for in both cases the resonator undergoes a slight change. In *OH*, there is a modification in the direction of *ŏŏ*, and in *AY*, in the direction of *ĭ*. This diphthongal character is essential in both cases but must not be exaggerated. The vowels from 1 to 5 may be termed lip vowels, since they are principally effected by varying degrees of lip rounding, and the series 5 to 12 are tongue vowels, in that they are differentiated by the varying degrees of tongue raising.

LONG AND SHORT VOWELS
There is one further point to be mentioned. Those printed in capitals are the so-called long or main vowels; and those in smaller type the so-called short or subordinate vowels. The terms long and short are applicable only when the vowels are pronounced in isolation, or with identical surrounding sounds, since the length of any vowel is influenced by its position in a word, and by the sounds which follow it. All vowels are of equal importance, whereas the terminology of main and subordinate would seem to indicate otherwise. These terms, however, will be retained, since they do imply certain characteristics which are important in exercises; for instance, the vowels denoted by capitals may be prolonged, whereas the remainder tend to lose their character when so treated.

There is one simple vowel which does not figure in the scale. This is the so-called neutral vowel, which is heard only in unstressed positions, 'ascribe, parliament, method.' The pitch of this sound lies approximately between that of *ER* and *ŭ*. In final positions, this vowel must never be so open that it approximates to *u*.

SUSTAINED TONE
The sequence of whispered resonances produces what has been called the resonator scale, which is the means by which tone is developed through the natural working of the resonator. Its expansion is first gained by the open jaw and forward tongue which open up the back of the throat. Its expansion is increased, principally indirectly, through the use of rib-reserve breathing, which induces full pharyngeal expansion.

Our aim, so far, has been to expand the resonator, and to acquire the ability to form the shapes of the vowels, and the ability to pass from one to the other without any alteration in the size of the resonator as a whole. The relative size of the two cavities varies but not the sum total size.

In developing resonance by means of this scale, we ultimately hear the tone as an unchanging, constant factor, brought about by our general bodily attitude towards the resonator, which by its open expansion imparts a full, rich quality. The tone, that is to say, is sustained irrespective of the shape, and is equally distributed throughout the whole range of these simple vowels. If this condition is not arrived at, a deterioration of the tone may always be heard in passing from the lip vowels to the tongue vowels.

We may here distinguish a difference between the function of the two main resonating cavities. The mouth is primarily concerned with imparting the character of the vowel to the tone, while the pharynx is concerned entirely with imparting sonority to the note, and does not exercise a selective faculty comparable to that possessed by the mouth.

THE IMPORTANCE OF POSTURE

It is in this connection that posture of the body is of such importance, for it is only by an absence of muscular constriction in a correctly poised body, that rib-reserve can effectually be attained, and it is rib-reserve breathing that supplies the answer to pharyngeal expansion, to which there is no short cut. To gain sonority by other means is to sacrifice the placing of the tone to the sonority, and thus to lose that balance between the resonating properties of the two cavities to which attention has already been drawn. A case in point is when the larynx is forced down from above by muscular tension at the base of the tongue. This does gain sonority, but only at the expense of the 'placing' of the tone, which becomes thick, throaty, and muffled. It is the full expansion of the pharynx from below which enables the vowel to be placed far forward in the mouth, thus giving a light, clear, ringing character to the vowel through 'top' resonance, while the fullness of the tone comes principally from the 'under' tone, or lower resonance, which results from pharyngeal expansion. In this way the vowels are perfected through their resonant properties, and the basic or general tone is developed.

One further feature of the scale remains to be noted. With three exceptions, all the pitches of the vowels are acoustically equidistant. It is this even spacing of their resonant notes which enables a clear and distinct differentiation to be made between them.

MOVEMENT AND TONE

The concept of utterance which leans to the view that sounds are strung together to form syllables, and that syllables are strung together to form words, and that words are strung together to form phrases, is destructive of rhythmic ease in speaking. The rejection of this attitude of mind brings us back to the idea of utterance as an alliance between tone and movement, to which reference has already been made. If proof of the validity of this view were needed, the resonator scale supplies the answer. By perfecting the vowels through their resonant properties, we set up a 'line' of tone which is heard as a constant factor and is the direct result of maintaining the cavities at a constant size. The tone does not vary from vowel to vowel, as it is the product of the musical function of the resonator. On the other hand, in practising the scale we change the shape of the mouth thirteen times. By so doing, we impress the character of the vowels on the tone, and thus make prominent the linguistic function of the resonator. This stream of moulded tone is further modified by articulatory movement into the consonants of a language. The complex of tone and movement is constantly varied by a continually changing pattern of stress and volume, pitch and inflection, in response to the logical and emotional states which the actor is called upon to portray, and is 'coloured' still further when the tone sensitively responds to the emotions experienced.

When the principles upon which the scale is founded are grasped it is necessary to link posture, breathing, and the conditions conducive to good tone, as ultimately all three are inseparable and react beneficially on each other. The relation of correct posture to breathing has been pointed out, but it is especially important to pay attention to the way in which the head is held on the shoulders, as tone cannot be developed if this is incorrect.

COMMON PROBLEMS WITH POSTURE

The position of the head most frequently seen is one in which it is poked forward in such a way as to restrict the resonator. This position is usually wrongly corrected by throwing up the chin, which results in the opposite fault, and successfully produces a state of tension in the throat. Another fault is a position in which the whole chest is thrown out and the head held back in a stiffened 'military' attitude. Yet another is when the shoulder blades are forced back as if in the endeavour to make them meet.

Correct posture and the correct carriage of the head may be helped by the following exercises. As in the exercises on relaxation, the object is to induce an awareness of the way in which the body is being held and there is little value in the exercises as such unless they are used as a means to this end.

EXERCISE TO ESTABLISH BASIC POSTURE

Stand with the back against, but not touching, a wall with the heels two inches out from the wall and with the feet some eighteen inches apart. Next, recall the sense of ease and relaxation associated with the supine position so that one feels equally at ease in the standing position. The arms should hang loosely, but not heavily, from the shoulders, and the knees should be straight but not braced back. Then allow the whole trunk to move back from the ankles until the back is touching the wall. The buttocks and the shoulders should reach the wall simultaneously. In this position, ideally, the spine should be nearly flat against the wall, the exception being in the lumbar spine, where it should be possible to pass the fingers between the wall and the back. The shoulders should be allowed to flatten out against the wall, but should not be forced back. The head should be directed forwards and upwards. This is a mental direction given to the head, which should be balanced easily with the eyes held level and with the chin neither tilted up nor drooping down. If the back of the head touches the wall, the position is incorrect. Allow the head to turn easily from side to side so that it does not become fixed. In this position, without allowing the back to come away from the wall and without raising the heels, slide the knees over the toes so that the back travels down the wall some twelve inches. As this occurs, the part of the lumbar spine which was not previously touching the wall should gradually make contact with it. The sensation should be that the head remains up while the knees travel forward. To resume the former position, try to feel that it is the head which moves up while the rest of the body follows and that one does not push oneself up from the feet. Do this several times to memorize the position of the back. Then, without pushing oneself away from the wall, wait until the balance of the body is restored as the body moves away from the wall in a straight line from the heels to the top of the head.

EXERCISES LINKING TONE AND RELAXATION

We are now in a position to attempt to link up relaxation, posture, and breathing with the development of tone. The exercise on pages

31–32 should be repeated, and then extended to cover the subordinate vowels. One should be aware of carrying out all the movements involved according to definite principles. The new pattern of movement should be sensed.

Exercise 1

HAH H́OO. HAH H́o͞o. HAH H́OH. HAH H́AW. HAH H́ŏ.
HAH H́AH. HAH H́ŭ. HAH H́ER. HAH H́ă. HAH H́ĕ. HAH H́AY.
HAH H́ĭ. HAH H́EE.

Exercise 2

The subordinate vowels are then treated in the same fashion.

HAH H́ĭ HAH H́o͞o HAH H́ĭ HAH H́o͞o HAH H́ĭ HAH H́o͞o, etc.
HAH H́ĕ HAH H́OH HAH H́ĕ HAH H́OH HAH H́ĕ HAH H́OH, etc.
HAH H́ă HAH H́ŏ HAH H́ă HAH H́ŏ HAH H́ă HAH H́ŏ, etc.
HAH H́ER HAH H́ŭ HAH H́ER HAH H́ŭ HAH H́ER HAH H́ŭ, etc.

Exercise 3

The following verses should first be whispered, then intoned, and, finally, spoken. Initiate the utterance from the diaphragm, falling back on the reserve breath when necessary. This applies especially to the final examples.

Row us out from Desenzano, to your Sirmione row!
So they row'd, and there we landed – "O venusta Sirmio!"
There to me thro' all the groves of olive in the summer glow,
There beneath the Roman ruin where the purple flowers grow,
Came that "Ave atque Vale" of the Poet's hopeless woe,
Tenderest of Roman poets nineteen hundred years ago,
"Frater Ave atque Vale" – as we wander'd to and fro
Gazing at the Lydian laughter of the Garda lake below
Sweet Catullus's all-but-island, olive-silvery Sirmio!
(*Frater Ave Atque Vale* – Lord Tennyson)

All along the valley, stream that flashest white,
Deepening thy voice with the deepening of the night,
All along the valley, where thy waters flow,
I walk'd with one I loved two and thirty years ago.
All along the valley while I walk'd to-day,
The two and thirty years were a mist that rolls away;

For all along the valley, down thy rocky bed,
Thy living voice to me was as the voice of the dead,
And all along the valley, by rock and cave and tree,
The voice of the dead was a living voice to me.

(*In the Valley of Cauteretz* – Lord Tennyson.)

Over the mountain aloft ran a rush and a roll and a roaring;
Downward the breeze came indignant, and leapt with a howl to
   the water,
Roaring in cranny and crag, till the pillars and defts of the basalt
Rang like a god-swept Iyre, and her brain grew mad with the
   noises;
Crashing and lapping of waters, and sighing and tossing of
   weed-beds,
Gurgle and whisper and hiss of the foam, while thundering surges
Boomed in the wave-worn halls, as they champed at the roots of
   the mountain.
Hour after hour in the darkness the wind rushed fierce to the
   landward,
Drenching the maiden with spray; she shivering, weary and
   drooping,
Stood with her heart full of thoughts, till the foam crests gleamed
   in the twilight,
Leaping and laughing around, and the east grew red with the
   dawning.

(*Andromeda* – Charles Kingsley.)

Now I will do nothing but listen,
To accrue what I hear into this song, to let sounds contribute
   towards it.
I hear bravuras of birds, bustle of growing wheat, gossip of flames,
   clack of sticks cooking my meals,
I hear the sound I love, the sound of the human voice,
I hear all sounds running together combined, fused or following
Sounds of the city and sounds out of the city, sounds of the day
   and night,
Talkative young ones to those that like them, the loud laugh of
   workpeople at their meals,
The angry base of disjointed friendship, the faint tones of the sick,

The judge with hands tight to the desk, his pallid lips
    pronouncing a death-sentence,
The heave'e'yo of stevedores unlading ships by the wharves, the
    refrain of the anchor-lifters,
The ring of alarm bells, the cry of fire, the whirr of swift-
    streaking engines and hose carts with premonitory tinkles
    and coloured lights.
The steam-whistle, the solid roll of the train of approaching cars,
The slow march play'd at the head of the association marching
    two and two,
(They go to guard some corpses, the flag-tops are draped with
    black muslin).
(Song of Myself – Walt Whitman.)

NASAL RESONANCE

Up to this point the nasal resonator has been somewhat cursorily dismissed when tone has been under discussion, and yet the power of the nose as a resonator is very considerable. Nasal resonance must never be allowed to predominate, but when the two main cavities of mouth and neck are fully expanded, nasal resonance may be present in the form of an added richness and helps to impart to the voice a ringing vibrant quality. In developing nasal resonance, it is imperative to bear in mind the necessity for preserving a balance in tone between the main cavities and the nose itself.

REASONS FOR NASALITY

If, for some reason, this balance between the main cavities and the nose is not achieved, the condition known as nasality is present. If this exists as a constant factor, or merely on vowel sounds in the proximity of nasal consonants, it is a fault in production. Nasality may sometimes be present as the result of insufficient expansion of the main cavities so that the resonance of the nose predominates. If this is so, it is usually eradicated in the course of training, when full expansion of the pharynx and mouth has been obtained. In this way the nose resonance is, as it were, absorbed by the resonance of the other two cavities One of the characteristics of the habitually nasal speaker is an apparent inability to open the jaw and throat. The importance of so doing is now seen to be more imperative than ever.

On the other hand, nasality often persists, even when the jaw is open and the mouth and pharynx are being fully used. This is

explained by the inability of the speaker to raise the soft palate sufficiently vigorously and thus to close the entrance to the naso-
pharynx and nose proper. The remedy for this is to train the ear to
detect the nasal quality, and at the same time to develop greater
muscular activity in the soft palate.

Yet another form of nasality results from excessive tension of the
muscles of the palate, often spreading to such an extent that the
tension can be seen in the nostrils. This imparts a hard, metallic
quality which is the distinguishing feature of nasal 'twang.' In
reality, it is the result of complete absence of true nasal resonance. It
is the pinching, tightening condition which is the cause of this.

ABSENCE OF NASAL RESONANCE

'Speakig through the dose' is yet another type, and is associated with
either a temporary or a permanent cold in the head. This, again,
indicates complete absence of nasal resonance and is the result of
congestion and blockage.

HOW TO OBTAIN NASAL RESONANCE

Nasal resonance may best be obtained by alternating nasal consonants and vowels. *M* is the most satisfactory for this purpose. In
forming the *M* the lips, as we have seen, are brought lightly together
over the open jaw. The lips must not be pursed or tightened in any
way. The tongue is to lie flat on the floor of the mouth as for *AH*. A
note is now sung, the sensation being that the vibrations of the note
are sent directly on to the closed lips which should tingle markedly.
If the lips are plucked apart by a finger, the tone is heard to be full
and clear as it issues from the mouth. If, on plucking the lips apart,
the resultant sound is dead and muffled, the result is not that
intended, and is probably due to closing the jaw and bunching up
the tongue, and thereby filling the mouth.

When the *M* can be easily made in this manner, the hands should
be cupped over the mouth and nose, and *M* and *AH* should be alternated. The rest of the main vowels should then be similarly treated.
There should be no break in the sound.

M AH M AH M AH M AH M AH M AH M AH M AH M AH

The vibrations for the consonant should be felt strongly on the
fingers and in passing from the *M* to the vowel a trace of this vibration, but only a trace, should remain. The ear, however, must be the

final arbiter in controlling the amount of nasal resonance which is present. It is also profitable to listen to nasal resonance from within by closing each ear by pressure of the fingers and repeating the above exercise. Only the faintest trace of nasal resonance must be heard on the vowels.

EXERCISES FOR NASAL RESONANCE
These words are then repeated one after the other on a continuous note, and in so doing a continuous hum or buzz is to be set up.

Exercise 1
mummy mummy mummy mummy mummy mummy mummy
ninny ninny ninny ninny ninny ninny ninny
money money money money money money money
memory memory memory memory memory memory memory
niminy niminy niminy niminy niminy niminy niminy
Remember the money, remember the money, remember the
    money, remember.

Exercise 2
Naomi remembered that June night, when the moon shone on the town and the moor, as she wandered aimlessly towards the ruined mansion, framed against a background of elms. Peering through a mullioned window, the moon glinted on the money the mad Mannering was fingering and counting.

Exercise 3
How sweet it were, hearing the downward stream,
With half-shut eyes ever to seem
Falling asleep in a half-dream!
To dream and dream, like yonder amber light,
Which will not leave the myrrh-bush on the height; . . .
To watch the crisping ripples on the beach,
And tender curving lines of creamy spray;
To lend our hearts and spirits wholly
To the influence of mild-minded melancholy;
To muse and brood and live again in memory,
With those old faces of our infancy
Heap'd over with a mound of grass,
Two handfuls of white dust, shut in an urn of brass!
                (*Song of the Lotus-eaters* – Lord Tennyson.)

Exercise 4

From harmony, from heavenly harmony,
   This universal frame began:
  When nature underneath a heap
   Of jarring atoms lay,
And could not heave her head,
The tuneful voice was heard from high,
'Arise, ye more than dead!'
Then cold, and hot, and moist, and dry,
In order to their stations leap,
And Music's power obey.
From harmony, from heavenly harmony,
   This universal frame began:
   From harmony to harmony
Through all the compass of the notes it ran,
The diapason closing full in Man.
           (*A Song for St. Cecilia's Day* – John Dryden.)

EXERCISING THE SOFT PALATE

To correct nasality arising from insufficient activity of the soft palate, it is necessary to recognize the sensation accompanying the high arching of the palate. This may best be done by whistling a sustained low note. Unless the entrance to the nose is closed, this cannot be done. Another way is to yawn. The soft palate will then rise quite definitely to close the entrance to the nose. One should then endeavour to retain the soft palate in this arched position while slowly allowing the mouth to resume its normal condition. In addition, hold the lips very loosely together and barely touching and breathe out sufficiently vigorously to cause them to vibrate. This cannot be done if the soft palate is not raised.

Exercise 1

Alternate *NG* and *AH*. For this exercise, the jaw is to be fully opened and the whispered breath is to be used. The breath is to be taken in through the nose with the tongue in the *NG* position. This sounds rather complicated. All one has to do, however, is to assume the position for *NG* silently, and breathe in whilst maintaining the position. The breath is to be exhaled strongly on *AH*. On repeating these sounds continuously one after the other, one is able to hear a slight clicking sound as the soft palate rises and the tongue is lowered to the position for the vowel. This resembles, but is not quite so strong as, a *K*. This slight K is to be made as clear as possible.

Exercise 2

NG ÁH NG ÁH NG ÁH NG ÁH NG ÁH NG ÁH

Repeat with *OO* and *EE*.

Exercise 3

In the following words the final consonant should first be detached from the preceding sounds and the pause between the two gradually shortened whilst carefully noting that no nasality is heard until the final nasal consonant is reached –

| ti ... me | ti .. me | time | n .. i .. ne | n . i . ne | nine |
| tow ... n | tow .. n | town | m .. i .. me | m . i . me | mime |

and with any words in which similar conditions obtain.

Exercise 4

Articulate the following with extreme clarity on all the nasals –

In the beginning she was singing while he was bringing the ripping dripping. Later he was tinkering and sprinkling with the blinking watering can, while she was tacking and hacking at the black lining of a hunting jacket.

Like a rocket shot to a ship ashore
The lean red bolt of his body tore,
Like a ripple of wind running swift on grass;
Like a shadow on wheat when a cloud blows past,
Like a turn at the buoy in a cutter sailing
When the bright green gleam lips white at the railing,
Like the April snake whipping back to sheath,
Like the gannet's hurtle on fish beneath,
Like a kestrel chasing, like a sickle reaping,
Like all things swooping, like all things sweeping,
Like a hound for stay, like a stag for swift,
With his shadow beside like a spinning drift.
(Reynard the Fox – John Masefield.)

It was eight bells ringing,
  For the morning watch was done,
And the gunner's lads were singing,
  As they polished every gun.
It was eight bells ringing,
And the gunner's lads were singing,
For the ship she rode a-swinging,
  As they polished every gun.
              (*The Fighting Temeraire* – Sir Henry Newbolt.)

Nasality resulting from tension is best tackled by using the exercises given to encourage nasal resonance. The lines should be spoken dreamily and slowly, exacting full value from the 'm's' and 'n's' and taking special care to relax the facial muscles against the background of a relaxed posture.

4 • THE NOTE

Our method of procedure, so far, has been that of the craftsman who fashions an instrument in such a way that the skilled executant is enabled to evoke the most aesthetically satisfying tone of which the instrument is capable. It is to this end that the separation of the vibrator and resonator is necessary. By examining and developing the resonator on its own merits by means of the whispered voice, we have prepared the way for the introduction of the element of note, so that this may be reinforced and amplified to the full by the open, expanded resonator.

We have also seen that one way in which the vocal instrument may be played is by means of changing the shape of the resonator without materially affecting its size. In so doing we produce vowels which are at the same time similar and dissimilar. Similar in that their general quality or tone is constant, and dissimilar in that their specific quality or vowel tone is variable.

But the playing of an instrument is thought of principally in connection with the variations which become possible by the introduction of the element of pitch. It has already been made clear that there is not much point in considering this aspect of an instrument or of the voice unless the notes of varying pitches can first be satisfactorily resonated.

THE VOCAL CORDS

For practical purposes a detailed knowledge of the structure of the larynx is entirely unnecessary, as it would be of no assistance in developing the action of the cords which can be influenced only by indirect means.

The term 'vocal cord' is unfortunate, in that it suggests two strings slung across the top of the windpipe. A truer, but rough, picture can be gained by imagining a tube, closed at one end by a flexible covering which is slit along its diameter. We should imagine the front of the slit as fixed, and the back ends as movable and free. The two edges of the slit represent the vocal cords. The edges, when seen from above, appear as two white bands stretched across the throat, the fixed ends being in the front and the movable ends at the back. These white bands are the actual vocal cords, which are composed of elastic tissue. When we breathe in, the free ends of the slit are drawn away from each other by muscular action. When we breathe out, they move closer together, and when we vocalize, they meet, closing the slit completely.

PRODUCING THE NOTE

When the cords are brought together the air is thereby completely boxed up, and can escape only by causing the edges of the slit to open. When we begin to breathe out, the pressure of the air inside the lungs is increased, making it possible for the breath to overcome the resistance offered to it by the closed cords, which are then moved apart. Because they are elastic, they spring together again, and the slit closes. Again they are parted, as breath pressure accumulates, and again they spring towards each other. It is the rhythmical opening and shutting of the slit which has the effect of cutting the breath stream up into a series of minute puffs which give rise to a musical note. The rapidity of the movement of the cords determines the pitch of the note; the interval of an octave, for example, is obtained by doubling, or halving, the number of times the cords part in a second of time.

VOICE TYPES

The length and mass of the cords determine the voice type. Thus, the bass voice will have longer, thicker cords than the baritone, and the tenor's cords may not be so long as those of the baritone. Similar differences account for the different types met with in women's voices. The lower voice of the man is also partially explained by the slightly longer and thicker cords he possesses, compared with those of the woman.

In discussing the note we have to consider –
1. The way in which it is set up or 'attacked,' its continuity, and the way in which it is terminated.
2. The compass or range of notes which may be demanded of the voice in portraying character and in meeting the demands of situation.

The closing and opening of the vocal cords and the rate at which this occurs is instinctive, and must remain so. The infant does not have to learn to cry. It expresses its disapproval of being born only too easily and, probably, too often! We do not have to learn how to bring the vocal cords together.

DURATION OF NOTE

Whenever we breathe out, the vocal cords move towards each other. In speaking and singing the mere desire to speak or sing is sufficient to bring the cords into contact with each other and to close the slit. Thus the vowel *AH* can be alternately whispered and vocalized, and we remain unconscious of the process, apart from the desire to alternate them. The note will last as long as we wish, always providing the breath supply is sufficient. The note will cease immediately we cease breathing out or pause in order to replenish the breath, and the cords will swing wide apart so that the intake is noiseless. The breath, in other words, is responsible for bringing the cords together, and also for the duration and cessation of the note. The cords will function perfectly, providing their natural action is not tampered with and we make no attempt to become conscious of the movements taking place in the larynx. If, however, there is imperfect co-ordination between the breathing muscles and those responsible for bringing the cords together, the attack of the note will be incorrect.

CORRECT ATTACK

Correct attack is the result of perfect timing between these two sets of muscles. The note must begin at the instant we start breathing out. In this way the cords are, as it were, brought into the breath stream.

THE GLOTTAL STOP

If, however, the timing is faulty, the slit closes too soon, in which case the cords are separated violently before the note begins. The effect of this is to prefix each note by a hard, clicking sound, known as a glottal stop.

This hard, 'glottal' attack is fortunately simple to overcome, but where the habit exists it is often most persistent. To guard against its occurrence, all initial work on vocalization should begin with an *H* sound, so that the responsibility of the breath for the attack of the note is inculcated. When the sense of starting the note on the breath has been acquired, the *H* may be lessened in duration and eventually dispensed with.

INCORRECT ENDING

A vowel which is sustained may be terminated abruptly by a tightening in the throat, in which case a sharp clicking sound would be heard to end the note. This is much more likely to occur in singing whenever vowels have to be sung *forte* at the top of the compass, but it is sometimes heard when a vowel is sustained in the course of developing the speaking voice. It may be avoided by breathing in when the note is to cease.

BREATHY QUALITY

The note should, in all normal circumstances, be full and clear with no trace of a woolly or breathy quality. If it is present, it should be noted whether the breath is being drawn in to the base of the lungs and whether shallow breathing, which is the result of expanding the upper part of the thorax, is not a contributory cause. The breath should pass out firmly but slowly from the base of the lungs and the ribs should not be allowed to collapse. The note should be attacked strongly at the instant exhalation begins, and the vowel which is to be sung should be prefixed by an *M*. The *M* sound is to be sustained for an appreciable time, and the lips are to be opened directly on to the vowel. While singing the *M*, the vibrations should be felt strongly upon the lips. It is not possible to go further than this in writing of this condition, which is often difficult to eradicate, and is the reverse of that which is essential for true clarity of utterance.

HEARING THE NOTE

The ear is responsible for the pitch of the note, and, therefore, for bringing about the complex movements in the larynx which enable the pitch to be varied. To reproduce a note of a given pitch, all that is necessary is that it should be correctly heard. Into the marvellous intricacies which explain the way in which this is done, we need not enter. If the sense of pitch is defective, it is impossible correctly to reproduce a given note. This situation can be remedied only by ear training and by concentrating on a clear mental 'picture' of the note in the mind at the instant it is to be reproduced.

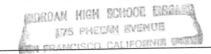

If the note is defective in any way, it will be noticeable, since the resonator of the voice does not possess the power of completely altering the note, as is the case with some instruments, but only of modifying it. We can now say that perfection of voice demands not only perfection of resonance but also perfection in the way in which the note is attacked and sustained.

THE TREMOLO

In sustaining a vowel, unsteadiness of pitch is frequently heard. This does not refer to the inability to hear the pitch of a note which results in singing flat or sharp, but to minute variations in frequency throughout the duration of a note which produces the effect known as tremolo. Of greater importance in singing where vowels are sustained beyond their normal duration, it can, nevertheless, frequently be detected in spoken passages when these are taken at a slow pace. This unsteadiness serves no purpose except to call attention to itself and is irritating to the ear when its presence is marked. To eradicate this fault care should be taken that the breath pressure is firm and constant. The ear, by concentrating on the desired note, should keep the pitch true. It is often a help to imagine that the note proceeds along a perfectly horizontal line with no deviation above it or below.

THE 'CENTRE' NOTE

Before bringing the vibrator and resonator into association, it is necessary to decide on the best pitch to use for practice. This will be one which lies towards the middle of the speaker's compass. This 'centre' note may easily be ascertained by first singing down the scale until the lowest note which can be sung is reached. Sung, not growled! An octave above this will give a note towards the middle of the voice, and this, or a note slightly below, should be used in the first place for all vocalization exercises.

Every actor should be aware of their centre note, as the bulk of their work will involve the middle part of the voice. In the course of time the sense of where to pitch the voice becomes instinctive. This is always important, especially when delivering a major speech of some length. In this case the voice should not be pitched too high at the beginning, which might make it impossible effectively to reach the notes demanded by an emotional climax, or to reach the pitch which a particular situation might demand.

AVERAGE CENTRE NOTE

The average centre notes for the voice types which are customarily distinguished are given below, although, as pointed out above, the centre note of the individual's voice may be readily ascertained.

A guide to the centre note

NOTE: there will be variations between individuals.

RESONANT AND DICTATED PITCH

When singing the vowels, the resonant pitch is no longer heard as such because the vocal note is the stronger of the two. It is the greater strength of the vocal note which makes it possible to sing any vowel on any pitch within a given compass. But the effect of the resonant pitches on the note is made audible in the richness of the resultant tone. This may be clearly heard by a simple experiment on the vowel *EE*. This is to be sung on the same pitch throughout. The jaw is first closed, but not clenched, and the lips are spread, and the vowel is sung. The jaw then remains closed, but the lips are relaxed, and the vowel is sung. Finally, the jaw is opened, and the loose lip position retained, and the vowel is sung. A marked improvement in resonation is noticed each time the position for the vowel is improved. The explanation of this may be understood if the experiment is repeated by means of the breath alone. A distinct lowering of the resonant note is heard as the expansion of the cavities is increased. It is in this way that every note which is sung is given maximum resonation by means of the notes on the resonator scale.

Exercise 1

In the correct *AH* position, a breath is passed through the cavities, attention being paid to the whispered pitch and the complete absence of constriction, which, if present, would be heard in the form of a rasping, scraping quality of breath. The note which is to be sung is then played, or heard mentally, and reproduced prefixed by an *H*. The breath pressure is to be firm and constant throughout the duration of the note which is to begin at the instant of breathing out and neither before nor after, and to cease before any sensation of breath shortage is experienced. The pitch of the note is to remain 'true' from start to finish and there must be no suggestion of a tremolo.

Exercise 2

In the easy, poised position, with rib-reserve breathing, each of the following vowels is first to be whispered. The whispered pitch should be checked, and also whether the resonator is free from constriction and fully open. The centre note is then introduced, prefixed by an *H* and terrninated by a fresh intake of breath represented by the final *H*.

H   AH – centre note – AH H.
H   OO – centre note – OO H.
H   EE – centre note – EE H.

Exercise 3

The following pairs of vowels are then to be sung on the centre note, one breath being used for each pair –

H A͡H OO, H A͡H OO, H A͡H OO, H A͡H OO.
H A͡H EE, H A͡H EE, H A͡H EE, H A͡H EE.
H O͡O EE, H O͡O EE, H O͡O EE, H O͡O EE.

Exercise 4

In the same way proceed to the following –

H A͡H OO E͡E, H A͡H OO E͡E, H A͡H OO E͡E.
H A͡H EE O͡O, H A͡H EE O͡O, H A͡H EE O͡O.
H O͡O AH E͡E, H O͡O AH E͡E, H O͡O AH E͡E.
H O͡O EE A͡H, H O͡O EE A͡H, H O͡O EE A͡H.
H E͡E AH O͡O, H E͡E AH O͡O, H E͡E AH O͡O.
H E͡E OO A͡H, H E͡E OO A͡H, H E͡E OO A͡H.

Exercise 5

Follow this with every vowel of the resonator scale prefixed by *HAH* using one breath, with ribs extended, for each pair.

Exercise 6

Repeat the scale, only this time omit the *H*. Repeat both exercises, but make the breath continuous.

A͡H OO A͡H o͝o A͡H OH A͡H AW A͡H ŏ A͡H AH A͡H ŭ A͡H ER A͡H ă
A͡H ĕ A͡H AY A͡H ĭ A͡H EE.

In all these exercises, if the resonator is functioning correctly, the tone will be full and clear and will not deteriorate in passing from one vowel to another. The sung note, if correct, will be effortlessly produced, and will remain constant in passing through any of the series of shapes.

COMPASS

In the establishment of tone up to this point, we have been principally concerned with obtaining satisfactory resonation for every vowel on a fixed note of the compass, and in maintaining an unbroken line of resonance so that the basic tone remains unimpaired, irrespective of the speech movements which are superimposed upon it. The tone, in other words, has been developed horizontally.

This is a fundamental condition of good voice production, but a great deal more is demanded of the actor's voice, which seldom, if ever, is sustained on one note for an appreciable time. The actor's voice must range over a whole series of notes which are determined, in the first instance, by the particular inflections required to speak a line and point its meaning. But the range of an inflection and the particular point of the compass at which it starts is determined principally by the emotional context of a situation in a play. If the tone is not to be impaired under these conditions, we must acquire the power of extending the range of the voice, and in so doing develop the tone vertically.

In normal conversation the voice is used round about its middle note and does not rise above or fall below this note to any marked extent. If this conversational range is not extended in both directions, the untrained voice will sound forced and strained whenever its upper limits have to be used.

FIXED RANGE

No-one has complete freedom where range is concerned, for the extreme limits to which the voice can rise and fall are more or less fixed when adolescence is reached. In other words, a high voice can rarely become a low voice, and vice versa, and the tone must be developed within the limits of the compass set by a particular voice. This is not to imply that range cannot be extended, for few speakers make use of all the notes of which their voices are capable. The essential point is the ability to produce free, open tone on all notes which lie within the compass.

No voice can be forced into a mould for which it was not designed. A person, therefore, who cannot speak low may tend to drive the voice down, and thus to throw the whole resonating system out of gear. When the voice is deemed too high and, when this is not merely because it is being pitched too high above its natural centre, much can be done to give the impression of lowness by attending to the tone.

TONE AND RANGE

The full open expansion of the resonator will give an impression of body and depth which will largely compensate for any lack of low notes in a particular voice. An illustration of what may be done has already been noted in the case of the vowel *EE*. When expansion is absent a thin, high effect is produced, whereas, if the same note be sung with maximum expansion of the cavities, the difference in resonation is marked, and the added sonority obtained has the effect, apparently, of lowering the pitch of the note.

It is usually the person with thin or otherwise indifferent tone who wishes to 'get the voice down.' A voice of whatever pitch will always be aesthetically satisfying so long as the tone itself is not meagre or otherwise defective.

MAINTAINING PLACEMENT

In the following exercises, it is the spoken vowel which is to be sustained. That is, the character of the vowel must not be sacrificed in order to gain fullness of tone, but must be kept well forward in the mouth, the richness and fullness being given to the notes entirely by the openness of the throat and the general expansion of the whole cavity. Special care is necessary to avoid any tightening when ascending the scale. When the highest notes are reached the sensation should be that they are being produced as effortlessly as the centre note. The higher the note, the more open and relaxed should one feel. In singing down, the tendency to make the lowest notes heavy, throaty, and 'thick' must be resisted. On the other hand, it is important to realize that to warble a series of notes, however charmingly, is of value to no-one. We must produce tone on the notes we sing, but be sure it is tone which suggests an enrichment of the speaking voice and not the 'fruity' backward placed tone which is associated with an unctuous pomposity.

EXERCISES FOR PITCH

All the precautions already detailed must be present to the mind. The good poise, the easy, erect carriage of the head, the open expanded throat, and the forward tongue. Every singing exercise is to be preceded by whispering the vowel which is to be sung, so that the resonating conditions may be heard to be at their best before the notes are introduced.

Exercise 1

HOO
HOH
HAW
HAH
HER
HAY
HEE

and then with

Hŏŏ
Hŏ
Hŭ
Hĕ
Hă
Hĭ

The scale given does not cover the range of notes which every actor should possess. One and a half octaves is the minimum requirement, but a really flexible voice will be able to range over two octaves with complete ease. In giving exercises for all who may read this book, it is impossible to be aware of any limitations in the reader's compass, so that this is really as far as it is safe to go in dealing with this matter on the printed page.

Exercise 2

For those who are certain the exercise given can be performed with perfect ease so that the highest note does not cause the slightest suspicion of strain, and the lowest note does not become a fruity growl, the starting note may be raised by a semi-tone and then lowered by a semi-tone which will develop the lower notes equally with the higher ones. Always providing the exercise can be performed with complete ease, it is safe to proceed in this way until two octaves can be covered, but it is pointless to force the notes at the extremes of the compass. Forcing prevents the voice from reaching the required notes; it not only becomes painful to listen to it, but it may be the means of causing irreparable damage to the voice.

The correct management of the note, and the easy, flexible distribution of the tone throughout the compass of the voice is the second of the main objectives which must be reached.

Exercise 3
Starting midway between one's 'centre' and lowest notes, the following lines should be intoned, raising the pitch by a semi-tone on each succeeding line. Be careful that the pitch of the note remains steady throughout the duration of each line and that the pitch does not drop. Give each line controlled support from the breath and initiate the voice from the diaphragm and see that the tone is clear and forward on the lips. There are additional examples on pages 43–4.

With eyes upraised, as one inspired,
Pale Melancholy sat retired;
And from her wild sequester'd seat,
In notes by distance made more sweet,
Pour'd through the mellow horn her pensive soul:
And dashing soft from rocks around,
Bubbling runnels joined the sound;
Through glades and glooms the mingled measure stole,
Or o'er some haunted stream, with fond delay,
Round a holy calm diffusing
Love of peace and lonely musing,
In hollow murmurs died away.

       (*The Passions* – William Collins.)

Exercise 4

These lines from G. K. Chesterton's '*Lepanto*' provide a good test of
the efficient management of all the elements so far discussed, and an
opportunity for vigorous articulation and control of volume of
tone. They should be spoken.

Dim drums throbbing, in the hills half heard,
Where only on a nameless throne a crownless prince has stirred,
Where, risen from a doubtful seat and half-attainted stall,
The last knight of Europe takes weapons from the wall,
The last and lingering troubadour to whom the bird has sung,
That once went singing southward when all the world was young,
In that enormous silence, tiny and unafraid,
Comes up along a winding road the noise of the Crusade.
Strong gongs groaning as the guns boom far,
Don John of Austria is going to the war,
Stiff flags straining in the night-blasts cold
In the gloom black-purple, in the glint old-gold,
Torchlight crimson on the copper kettle-drums,
Then the tuckets, then the trumpets, then the cannon,
    and he comes.
Don John laughing in the brave beard curled,
Spurning of his stirrups like the thrones of all the world,
Holding his head up for a flag of all the free.
Love-light of Spain – hurrah!
Death-light of Africa!
Don John of Austria
Is riding to the sea.

Further material is –

The Song of the Lotus-Eaters, Lord Tennyson.
Samson Agonistes (Messenger speech), John Milton.
Hippolytus (Messenger speech), John Milton.
Electra (Messenger speech), John Milton.
Richard III, v. iii. (Richmond: More than I have said), Shakespeare.
Henry VI, III. i. 4. (Queen Margaret: Brave warriors, Clifford and
Northumberland), Shakespeare.

5 · THE WORD

All the steps so far taken have been towards acquiring an unbroken line of tone, which is to be sustained through all the changes in the resonator resulting from the vowel shapes. We must now consider how these conditions are to be maintained in spite of the interruptions of the tone occasioned by the introduction of consonants. Whereas all vowels are the result of the passage of the note through the open resonator, the third and final modification of the breath stream is brought about by impeding the outward passage of the breath. This may be done by completely closing the resonator and then opening it, or by bringing the articulating organs close together so that the breath stream issues through a restricted opening.

TYPES OF CONSONANTS
Consonants differ from each other in five ways –

1. They may be voiced or voiceless.
2. They may be made in differing manners.
3. They may be made in different places.
4. Some demand a closed jaw, others a partially closed jaw, and some may be made with an open jaw.
5. They may vary in strength of articulation.

The main difference between the following pairs is that the first of each pair is voiceless and the second is voiced, i.e. the vocal cords are in vibration, and this is indicated by the straight and wavy lines beneath them. This distinction cannot be heard unless it is realized that the name and the sound of a consonant are two different things. Thus *f, v, z,* and *k* are called *eff, vee, zed* and *kay,* but their sounds can be heard without any accompanying vowel. In alternating the following pairs, the articulating organs must not be allowed to move –

F V F V F V F V F V F V

S Z S Z S Z S Z S Z S Z

PLACE OF ARTICULATION

If the sounds of *D, L, N, S,* are made, it will be noticed that they are made in the same place but that they differ in manner. Similarly with *G* and *NG.*

MANNER OF ARTICULATION

P, B, T, D, K, G, on the other hand, are all made in the same manner, but each pair is made in a different place.

The sounds *M, N, L, P, B, T, D, K, G, NG,* and *H* can all be made with an open jaw, although at this stage some may have difficulty in so doing, whereas *S, Z,* and the *SH* and *CH* sounds require a closed jaw.

In the tabulation shown opposite, the vertical columns indicate the way in which each sound is formed and the horizontal columns the place where they are formed. The first of each pair is voiceless and the second voiced.

Some of these consonants call for consideration here, since they are not consonants in the strict sense of the term and do not appear in any of the consonant exercises. They are *H, W,* and *Y.*

H

H does not demand any closure of the resonator whatever, as it is formed by the passage of the unvocalized breath through the vowel shapes. Before an *H* is heard the articulating organs take up the position for the following vowel. The shape is then breathed through for the *H.* The position of the organs does not then change, but the vocal cords come into vibration for the vowel. An *H,* in other words, could justifiably be considered more as an unvocalized vowel than a consonant. There are actually as many *H* sounds as there are vowels, although it is never necessary to distinguish between them. It is surprising to realize that there are voiced *H* sounds. These occur only when the *H* is between two vowels and are not in the consonantal repertoire of all speakers. Practice on *H* is not necessary as this will already have been undertaken in association with the vowel shapes. In 'He had his hat on his head,' the number of *Hs* which are pronounced depends upon the number of stresses and the speed at which the words are spoken. It is possible to speak this phrase perfectly correctly with only three of the *H* sounds made audible. To pronounce them all in all circumstances would sound highly unnatural.

Place of Formation	Manner of Formation						
	Complete Closures	*Partial Closures*					
	Explosives	Lateral	Nasal	Rolled and Tapped	Fricative	Semi-vowel
Open resonator					*H –*	
Two lips	*P B*		*– M*			*W*
Lower lip and upper teeth					*F V*	
Tongue-tip and teeth					*TH TH* [θ] [ð]	
Tongue-tip and upper gums	*T D*	*– L*	*– N*	*– R*	*S Z*	
Tongue blade and front of hard palate	*CH GE* [tʃ] [dʒ] (*church*) (judge)				*SH ZH* [ʃ] [ʒ] (rou*ge*)	
Front of tongue and hard palate						*– Y*
Back of tongue and soft palate	*K G*		*– NG* [ŋ]			

r – the untrilled English r is not shown on this chart as it is a frictionless sound

W AND Y

The consonants *W* and *Y* are very similar, acoustically, to vowel sounds. Nevertheless they are always regarded as consonants on *functional* grounds, i.e. they are always used, like consonants, at word and syllable boundaries.

W is a rapid voiced glide beginning approximately at the position for the *OO* sound.

Y is a rapid voiced glide beginning approximately at the position for *EE*.

Some speakers waste effort over the initial sound in 'when, where, why, what', etc. This particular sound has now lost currency and it is not necessary to make the distinction between voiced and unvoiced, unless to reinforce the onomatopaeic value of the words. Context will always ensure the distinction between such pairs as 'weather, whether'; 'way, whey'; 'which, witch.'

SOME COMMON PROBLEMS

The consonant table should give all the indication necessary as to the formation of the majority of these sounds, but some of them call for detailed examination owing to the difficulty experienced by many speakers when they come to be used in connected speech. These are the explosives, L sounds, R sounds, and the sibilants.

THE EXPLOSIVES – P, T, K; B, D, G

These consonants may be considered together, as they are all subject to the same errors in formation. All explosives are formed by imprisoning the air by completely closing the resonator at some point and then separating the articulating organs. The air, suddenly released, produces the slight explosive sound which is characteristic of these consonants. The escaping air necessarily continues for an appreciable time after the articulating organs have been separated. They cannot, therefore, be pronounced without an independent sound.

ASPIRATION

In the case of P, T, and K this independent sound is an H and in the case of B, D, and G it is a short form of the neutral vowel. This should be verified by repeating the consonants in pairs, i.e. P, B; T, D; K, G. The sound of the consonants must be given and not their names – not PEE, BEE; TEE, DEE; KAY, GEE. If the pairs are pronounced with a following vowel, it will be heard that the independent sound remains in the case of P, T, K, but that its place is taken by the following vowel in the other group, i.e. P^hAH, T^hAH, K^hAH, but BAH, DAH, GAH. P, T, K on this account are said to be aspirated. The degree of aspiration varies considerably from speaker to speaker. It should never be prominent to a marked degree, and to this end the articulating organs must be separated neatly and with rapidity. If they part slowly, the organs pass through the position of the corresponding fricative consonant and cause it to become audible. Thus 'tea for two' becomes 'tsea for tsoo.' Imagine a Ulysses who gave full bent to aspiration –

> Time hath, my lord, a wallet at his back,
> Wherein he puts alms for oblivion,
> A great sized monster of ingratitudes:
> Those scraps are good deeds past; which are devour'd
> As fast as they are made, forgot as soon
> As done: . . .
>
> (*Troilus and Cressida*, III. III.)

ABSENCE OF ASPIRATION

On the other hand, complete absence of aspiration is either comic or affected.

In practising *B*, *D*, *G*, in final positions, care must be taken to avoid an intrusive vowel, e.g. 'big^{er}, bad^{er}, dog^{er}'. This is the result of fully voicing these sounds which are always partially de-voiced when in final positions. They begin voiced and end breathed.

INCOMPLETE EXPLOSIVES

Not all explosives are completely articulated. When one is followed by another, only the stop of the first and the release of the second are heard. Compare 'gape, gaped; rob, robbed; look, looked; sag, sagged.' The same situation occurs when final and initial explosives are in juxtaposition, e.g. 'rhubarb pie, hot dog, black gloves.' In 'sit tight, glad day, ripe pears, herb broth, black cat, leg grip,' the pairs of consonants are identical but neither is complete, for we hear only the stop of the first and the release of the second. It is the length of the silence which gives the impression of two sounds. The stop, its duration, and its release must all be duly observed, otherwise the impression is of one sound only. Compare 'red ear, red deer.' The only difference between these two pairs is in the length of the stop. Some speakers, under the impression that they are gaining additional clarity, separate these and similar pairs, often with quite ludicrous effect. There is no occasion for this. To do so in a play which reproduces the conversational mode of speech would be absurd and a travesty of the truth.

NASAL AND LATERAL PLOSION

A vowel should not be inserted between an explosive and a

following nasal, e.g., 'cottn, muttn, rottn, buttn, hiddn, suddn,' and not 'cottun, muttun, rottun,' etc. The insertion of a vowel between an explosive and a following *L* is also unnecessary, e.g. 'littul' for 'little,' 'mortul' for 'mortl'.

EXERCISES FOR EXPLOSIVES

All the explosives may be practised in association with the vowels. Thus the vowel scale is used in this fashion –

Exercise 1

OOP POO OHP POH AWP PAW AHP PAH AYP PAY EEP PEE

OOB BOO OHB BOH AWB BAW AHB BAH AYB BAY EEB BEE

OOT TOO OHT TOH AWT TAW AHT TAH AYT TAY EET TEE

OOD DOO OHD DOH AWD DAW AHD DAH AYD DAY EED DEE

OOK KOO OHK KOH AWK KAW AHK KAH AYK KAY EEK KEE

OOG GOO OHG GOH AWG GAW AHG GAH AYG GAY EEG GEE

OOP BOO OHB POH AWT DAW AHD TAH AYK GAY EEG KEE,
    etc.

Exercise 2

When three explosives are in juxtaposition the question of treatment and clarity becomes more involved. In 'act two, sagged door; hope to, hoped to; rob doctor, robbed doctor; knock twice, knocked twice; bog down, bogged down,' separation of the respective pairs would result in 'act[h] two, hoped[h] to, knocked[h] twice and sagged[er] door, robbed[er] doctor, bogged[er] down,' which is ridiculous. The distinction between 'hope to' and 'hoped to' lies in the length of the stops for the *T* sounds, and this must be of the right duration to distinguish between the following pairs –

wrap ten	wrapped ten	pastimes	past times
scrub too	scrubbed too	buy toast	bite toast
cook dinner	cooked dinner	good answer	good dancer
rag Dora	ragged Dora	room eight	room mate

Exercise 3

On the other hand, 'wrapped parcels, escaped prisoner, scrubbed benches, bagged game, talked quietly, stopped barking, parked car, begged gifts,' can and should be separated. Example –

> Saturday was a sad day to wake up to. Not only a sad day, but a bad day, for Kate Pringle, our good cook, for the third time planned to leave us – and before breakfast too – and we had to catch the train at Great Batterton at eight ten. This entailed eight dreary miles in the old Dodge. Cook had downed tools on Friday at being asked to bake two fruit tarts of bottled black currants to follow the creamed cod and grilled chops. But my smart, pressed trousers and neatly tied tie made cook smile as with gloom graved deep on my brow, I took up the eight kippers for breakfast and prepared to cook them. 'You're past praying for,' said Kate. 'Cook kippers and all dressed up to kill?' So for the third time she stayed. We returned at night to find she had repented during the day and had planned a good meal of herb broth, roast pigeons, and rhubarb pie.

Exercise 4
The following may be taken as a test for aspiration –

> In Tooting two tutors astute,
> Tried to toot to a Duke on a flute,
> But duets so gruelling
> End only in duelling
> When tutors astute toot the flute.

THE GLOTTAL STOP
There is yet another explosive which is often heard but which is never indicated in the spelling of a word. It is known as the glottal stop, and is formed in the larynx by a closure of the vocal cords, much as a *P* is formed by the closure of the lips. It is represented by phoneticians by the symbol [ʔ] and the sound is regularly heard from many speakers. In extreme cases, it is used to replace the other explosive consonants, especially *P*, *T*, and *K*, and is a marked characteristic of a number of dialects. In such speakers a series of 'clicks' is substituted for the explosives. The difficulty does not lie in learning to acquire the correct sound, but in remembering to use it in preference to ʔ.

THE GLOTTAL BEFORE VOWELS
Again, many speakers prefix an initial vowel by the glottal stop as an

additional means of emphasis –

It's ?awful.

To eliminate this explosive it is necessary to intone a vowel, listening carefully to hear that the vowel is terminated by the closing consonant, and not by clicking the cords together. For this purpose all the exercises in vowels followed by *P*, *T*, and *K* should be used, both to eliminate the sound when it is substituted for an explosive and also in those cases when it is inserted before an explosive.

FORMATION OF L SOUNDS

Every *L* sound has a primary and a secondary articulation. In both popular varieties of *L* the primary articulation is the raising of the tongue tip to the upper gum ridge and the lowering of the sides. It is the secondary articulation which determines the difference between the two *L* sounds; known as 'clear' and 'dark' *L*. In the case of clear *L* the front part of the tongue, behind the tip, is raised towards the hard palate and gives the sound a slight 'i' resonance. During the formation of dark *L* the back of the tongue is raised towards the soft palate, as a secondary articulation, giving the sound a slight OO resonance.

USE OF CLEAR AND DARK L

Clear *L* is usually used before vowels and dark *L* before consonants, also at the ends of words. For example, clear *L* is heard in 'leave, alone, please' and dark *L* in 'old, pool, little.'

When in final positions, and when the next word begins with a vowel, the 'dark' *L* becomes 'clear.' Thus in 'orange peel' the *L* is 'dark,' but in 'Peel an orange' it is 'clear.'

In spite of the fact that the two *L*s are not interchangeable, some speakers use 'clear' *L* in final positions under the mistaken impression that this is an added refinement in speaking. It has the effect of making speech sound unreal and stilted. It may be noted in passing that the 'clear' *L* in final positions is one of the characteristics of Irish speech.

For many speakers *L* sounds are a source of great trouble. If the tongue is lazy, the tongue-tip articulation is omitted, in which case the *L* ceases to exist and a vowel of the o͞o type remains. In such cases 'till' becomes 'tio͞o', 'milk' becomes 'mio͞ok,' 'railway' becomes 'raio͞oway,' 'bell' becomes 'beo͞o,' and so on. Vigorous exercise of the

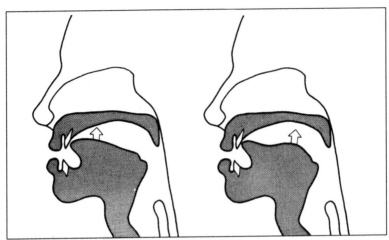

Fig.4 Formation of clear L (left) and dark L (right).

tongue tip will usually overcome this error.

Many speakers use a very 'dark' *L* and this, combined with general tongue laziness, drags the preceding vowel down to an incorrect position. In such cases 'field' becomes 'fiulled,' 'mail' becomes 'meull,' 'while' becomes 'whahl.' To overcome this an *L* with higher resonance must be obtained.

Exercise 1

With the tongue tip on the upper gums a series of *L*s should be pronounced, each having the resonance of the vowels from 5–12. This should be repeated until the secondary articulation of any of these *L*s can be assumed at will. The tongue tip must not leave the upper gums during this exercise, and the *L*s and the vowels are to be formed simultaneously, and may be represented thus –

$$L^{AH} \quad L^{\breve{u}} \quad L^{ER} \quad L^{\breve{a}} \quad L^{\breve{e}} \quad L^{AY} \quad L^{\breve{i}} \quad L^{EE}$$

The tongue tip articulation should be maintained through the sense of touch, and the position of the body of the tongue should be controlled by the ear. It is waste of time to try to feel what the rest of the tongue is doing. At first the exercise will sound more like a series of vowels than a series of *L*s, but with some adjustment both the *L* and the resonance of the vowel may be heard in equal proportions.

Exercise 2
When this can be done the *L* with *ER* resonance must be isolated and used to terminate all vowels.

AH	AH	L^{ER}	marl	ĕ	ĕ	L^{ER}	fell
ŭ	ŭ	L^{ER}	gull	AY	AY	L^{ER}	fail
ER	ER	L^{ER}	furl	ĭ	ĭ	L^{ER}	fill
ă	ă	L^{ER}	pal	EE	EE	L^{ER}	feel

A dark *L* is often heard from Scottish speakers in such words and phrases as 'will you, tell you, million, familiar, brilliant, pillion, scullion, Italian, Australian.'

When the formation of a vowel before *L* is incorrect, the correction of the resonance of the *L* will usually bring about a correction in the formation of the vowel, and it is generally a waste of time to tackle the vowel before the *L* has been corrected.

THE VOICELESS L
It has already been noted that there is no voiceless *L* in normal English although one is often heard as a speech defect for *S*. Voiceless *L* is a characteristic of Welsh, in which language it is represented by *ll* as in Llewellen. Shakespeare indicated this voiceless *L* by the *F* in 'Fluellen.'

COMPARING CLEAR AND DARK L
The following pairs of words may be practised for comparison and for obtaining a clear distinction between the two varieties –

Exercise 1

leap	peal	lop	poll
lip	pill	law	wall
lane	nail	loan	mole
lead	dell	look	pull
lap	pal	loot	tool
luck	cull	allow	owl
lurch	churl	lie	isle
lark	carl	alloy	oil

Exercise 2

While London Laughs is the title of a brilliant musical likely to draw, or almost pull, all the town when it is installed at the Plaza. The film sparkles with a wealth of lively, lilting lyrics in Val Carlyle's most powerful style. The eye is alternately regaled and, at intervals, almost assailed by really beautiful and enthralling scenes which ably fill the bill. I must not steal the thunder and indulge my liking for divulging the plot, and indeed cannot, for there is no denial that it was difficult to unravel. As a spectacle, the film is compelling, and culminates with Bucolic Frolic and Lido Love-tale. In the former, twelve festal vestals in purple and yellow farthingales girdled with myrtle leaves, revolve before a back cloth of rolling Alps and with rippling trills compete with a concealed chorus of pulsating nightingales. The latter is a bold, alluring spectacle inspired by Canaletto. 'Les Girls' exult in soulful strains as they float in gondolas along a real canal, illuminated by opal and emerald hues, to the full throated chorus of kilted gondoliers. This film is elsewhere described by several of my colleagues as puerile, juvenile, and infantile.

R SOUNDS

There is only one letter in the alphabet to represent the three varieties of this sound which are heard normally. Two others are heard as speech defects. The two most important members of this family of sounds are known as the frictionless or untrilled *R*, and the trilled or rolled *R*.

UNTRILLED R

Untrilled *R* is made by curling back the tip of the tongue in the proximity of the upper gums. It is the characteristic sound given to initial *R* by the great majority of speakers and is the only one possessed by many southerners.

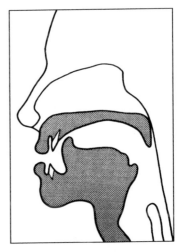

Fig. 5 Untrilled R – the most common R sound in English.

TRILLED R

Trilled *R* is made by a rapid succession of taps by the tongue tip against the upper gums. It is the sound regularly used in all positions by the majority of Scottish speakers.

TAPPED R

Tapped *R* is a near relative of trilled *R* and is made by one flick of the tongue tip against the upper gums.

COMMON PROBLEMS WITH R

Southern English speakers and those who follow them do not pronounce the *R* in all positions. It is always heard initially, but when final and when before consonants it is silent –

A he(r)d of red dee(r).
He(r).
He(r) book.

Many southern speakers employ the tapped *R* when it occurs between two vowels and also as a linking consonant when one word ends with an R and the following word begins with a vowel, e.g. –

Fathe(r), but father and mother.

Fa(r), but far and near.

He(re), but here it is.

Mo(re), but more and more.

In the West of England and in Ireland the untrilled *R* is pronounced in all positions. Often the curling back of the tongue is simultaneous with the formation of the vowel so that the vowel and the *R* coalesce. This is an expected characteristic in good American speech, and is known as retroflection.

The actor must be able to reproduce any of these *R* sounds at will, and use them in such a way as to render his speech both credible and acceptable, even to the native speaker whose speech habits he is reproducing.

LINKING R

The tapped *R* often links words together when one ends with an R and the other starts with a vowel. If the *R* is not used in these positions, an ugly hiatus results. It is essential when using this linking *R* that the stress should fall on the vowel of the following word to avoid turning her eyes into 'her reyes.' Many speakers are so terrified of doing this that they cut out the linking *R* altogether and so fail to make use of a consonant which aids smooth, legato delivery. What usually happens then is that a glottal explosive is inserted to prevent the two vowels from being run together. This is not only ugly, but unnecessary. This linking *R* is not used when the final syllable begins and ends with an *R*, e.g. 'deare(r) and dearer,' 'empero(r) and empress.'

ACQUIRING A ROLLED R

For those who wish to acquire a rolled *R*, great perseverance is necessary. All general exercises which employ the tongue tip are of value but in addition the syllables 'ter,' 'dah' should be repeated with considerable rapidity, forming the *T* sound on the teeth and the *D* in the usual place. This eventually results in a faint roll of the tongue tip.

Rolled *R* may also be acquired by trying to hold the tongue tip loosely in the proximity of the upper gums and breathing out very strongly so that the tip flutters.

INTRUSIVE R

When words ending in the vowels *ER, IER, AW*, are followed by an *R*, the *R* is silent when the words are final, or when followed by a consonant, but linking *R* is used when they are followed by words beginning with a vowel as we have seen –

He(r). He(r) book. Her eyes.
He(re). He(re) they are. Here it is.
Mo(re). Some mo(re) please. More and more.

Many words contain these same vowel sounds but have no *R* in their spelling. When they are followed by a word beginning with a vowel the tendency is incorrectly to insert an *R* –

Sofa.	Sofa R and chairs.	A gala R opening.
India.	India R and China.	The Infanta R of Spain.
Caw.	Caw R of the rook.	Nostalgia R and tears.

THE W SUBSTITUTE

The other defective *R* is more widely heard. It is the 'weath of vewy wed woses' sound, but is not really a *W*. The tongue is in the *OO* position and the lips are in the *V* position. The principal difficulty in its removal is the re-education of the tongue and remembering not to make use of the incorrect sound once the correct position has been established. If the tongue starts in the position of the medial consonant in 'measure, leisure, treasure,' it will be in the right position for *R*. This medial consonant should then be isolated and prolonged. When this can be done for a reasonable time, the tongue tip should be curled back whilst prolonging the sound. This will produce an untrilled *R* which will sound breathy and blurred, but once the position has been learnt it should be practised until the *R* becomes clear and defined. It will be necessary at first to dismiss the sound of *R* from the mind altogether. If this is not done, the stimulus will cause the articulating organs to assume their faulty positions. It will be especially important to resist the tendency of the lower lip to move up to the upper teeth. Another method is to insert the bent knuckle of the fore-finger under the tongue whilst pronouncing the medial consonant in 'measure.' When the position of the tongue has been learnt, it must be practised until it can be correctly assumed at will.

These remarks are made more for the benefit of those who wish to acquire this faulty *R* and who cannot do so by imitation, than for those who possess it already.

Exercise 1

'India is the place' remarked Gloria Ayles to me to-day. She and Aurora O'Malley are co-stars in *Oriental Revels*, a saga of fear shot amid the heat of Africa and India and the snows of China and Tibet. The Rajah is played by Jonah O'Dyer. The high spot comes when Gloria and Aurora are toying with vanilla ices to the faint strains of the Sonata in G, under an umbrella erected over a table on the piazza of the palace. From behind a bamboo sofa on their right, after gnawing a bone, a jaguar springs, and the paw of the beast is almost on Gloria as the Rajah appears to ward off the clutching claws and to restore law and order. Aurora is always expert in awe and sustains this scene well. But the idea of Gloria all red and raw in technicolour vanished as I thought of her glorious curls framed in a panama and veil on the placards of Poona and Putney.

Exercise 2
For once upon a raw and gusty day.

(*Julius Caesar,* I. ii.)

In awe of such a thing as I myself.

(*Ibid.*)

I speak too long; but 'tis to peize the time
To eke it, and to draw it out in length,
To stay you from election.

(*The Merchant of Venice,* III. ii.)

The attribute to awe and majesty.

(*The Merchant of Venice,* IV. i.)

Exercise 3
The actuary's honorary secretary showed her extraordinarily literary superiority by working literally solitarily in the library particularly regularly during February. Literary secretaries are fortunately a rarity.

Exercise 4
Contemporary literature literally littered the library table.

Exercise 5
The desultory plenipotentiary's interrogatory remarks were superogatory.

S AND Z
The sibilant nature of these consonants and their frequency of occurrence in English make it necessary to pay great attention to them. A perfect *S* depends not only upon the position of the tongue, but also upon the condition of the air channel through which the breath passes, and, possibly, upon dentition. Incorrect position of the tongue will, of course, result in a lisp. When the tongue tip is too far forward a lisp of the *TH* type is present. The other type of lisp results when the breath is allowed to flow over the sides of the tongue instead of over its tip, a type of voiceless *L* being substituted for *S.* The removal of such defects is imperative. Their removal is simple in theory, but the extremely fine adjustments which are

needed for the perfect S require great patience and are often most elusive.

FORMING S

If either of the speech defects exists, the tongue can be got into the right position for S from the T sound which should be present to the mind throughout the following exercise. If the S is present to the mind, the tongue will receive the wrong stimulus and will take up the position for the defective sound. The T should be pronounced extremely slowly, so that the tip is barely removed from the upper gums, whilst the sides of the tongue remain in contact with the upper teeth. Another method is to start from a whispered EE. Whilst continuing this the tongue tip should be raised until it is a fraction away from its correct position.

A satisfactory S may also be obtained by placing the tongue tip behind the lower teeth and raising the body of the tongue to approximate with the gum ridge. In order to avoid excessive sibilance, whichever formation you use, it is important to think and direct the air stream across the cutting edge of the front, upper teeth.

Even when the correct position of the tongue is habitual, there is great divergence between the S sounds which can be heard. The finer adjustments of the tip of the tongue, the size and shape of the air channel through which the breath flows, as well as the dentition, are then the determining factors.

CORRECTING FAULTS

To correct such faulty esses is a matter of adjusting the position of the body of the tongue and also its muscular tone until an S of the desired frequency results. That a perfect S is the result of correct frequency may easily be proved by making a series of S sounds on a rising scale of whispered notes. The lowest S of the scale will sound 'flat' and the highest will sound strident. If the S is flat, it often helps to make an S with the body of the tongue in the EE position, and if it is strident and whistles an attempt may be made to lower its frequency by making the sound with the body of the tongue in the ER position. But these are nothing more than rough guides which may be attempted in the absence of expert help.

ard tongue, in association with a feeling of openness in the
at, and the 'free' production of the centre note 'on the breath'.
connect these three vowels AY and AW are employed and the
lete exercise can be set out thus –

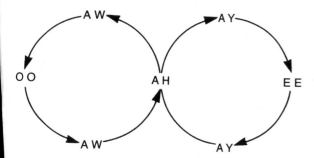

wel is first prefixed by an H, the exercise being made contin-
are must be taken to avoid spreading the lips on AY and EE.

e 2

his exercise can be done with ease, the vowels are prefixed by
his consonant, the lips are to meet lightly. They must not be
gether as in the formation of an explosive, but must be, as
brought together over the teeth, which must remain apart
ut the exercise. The usual way of forming an M is to close
nd bunch the tongue up in the mouth, which results in a
, muffled, dead M. With the open jaw and flat, forward
e vibrations are to be felt sufficiently to cause the lips to
is sensation of forward production can be increased by
at the whole of the sound is directed towards the closed
ot to the soft palate. The lips should be plucked apart by a
which case, if the M is being correctly made, the tone is
full and forward in the mouth. Each M is to be sustained
al duration with the vowels.

in precisely the same way as M, with the vibrations to
oth the tongue tip and upper teeth. The open jaw for
ant serves to bring home the fact that the tongue, in
ward and upwards, opens up the back of the mouth
cent effect, whereas with the closed jaw there is an
falling off of tone.

EXERCISES FOR S

When the desired S has been obtained it should be practised in
initial, final, and medial positions.

Exercise 1

The S should be prolonged before passing to the vowel, when the
first group is attempted, thus –

S	.	.	.	.	EE
S	.	.	.	.	ĭ
S	.	.	.	.	AY
S	.	.	.	.	ĕ

and so on with all the vowel sounds whilst gradually lessening the
duration of the S.

Exercise 2

All the vowels are then to be followed by S and afterwards by Z and
finally practised medially; neither consonant in these exercises is to
be prolonged –

EE	.	.	S		EE	.	.	Z
AY	.	.	S		AY	.	.	Z
AH	.	.	S		AH	.	.	Z
AW	.	.	S		AW	.	.	Z
OH	.	.	S		OH	.	.	Z
OO	.	.	S		OO	.	.	Z

Take great care to preserve the right degree of voice when final S
represents the Z sound. Many speakers devoice final Z completely
and so make their speech more sibilant than necessary.

Exercise 3

To be followed by S in consonantal groups –

SP OO,	SP OH,	SP AW,	SP AH,	SP AY,	SP EE.
ST OO,	ST OH,	ST AW,	ST AH,	ST AY,	ST EE.
SK OO,	SK OH,	SK AW,	SK AH,	SK AY,	SK EE.
SM OO,	SM OH,	SM AW,	SM AH,	SM AY,	SM EE.
SN OO,	SN OH,	SN AW,	SN AH,	SN AY,	SN EE.
SL OO,	SL OH,	SL AW,	SL AH,	SL AY,	SL EE.

OO SP,	OH SP,	AW SP,	AH SP,	AY SP,	EE SP.
OO ST,	OH ST,	AW ST,	AH ST,	AY ST,	ES ST.
OO SK,	OH SK,	AWSK,	AH SK,	AY SK,	EE SK.
OO SPS,	OH SPS,	AW SPS,	AH SPS,	AY SPS,	EE SPS.
OO STS,	OH STS	AW STS,	AH STS,	AY STS,	EE STS.
OO SKS,	OH SKS,	AW SKS,	AH SKS,	AY SKS,	EE SKS.

Exercise 4

All consonants have their value, and esses may be used in such a way that their aesthetic possibilities are exploited in the same way as those of *M*, *N*, and *L*, which are usually regarded as the more 'musical' consonants. Consider the opening quatrain of Keats's sonnet –

> It keeps eternal whisperings around
> Desolate shores, and with its mighty swell
> Gluts twice ten thousand caverns, till the spell
> Of Hecate leaves them their old shadowy sound.

With 'flat' or strident esses the beauty of such language will vanish even as it is uttered. If the following are not to become 'a very vile jingle of esses' they will 'ask some care in the true performing' of them –

> My gentle Puck, come hither. Thou remember'st
> Since once I sat upon a promontory
> And heard a mermaid, on a dolphin's back
> Uttering such dulcet and harmonious breath,
> That the rude sea grew civil at her song,
> And certain stars shot madly from their spheres,
> To hear the sea-maid's music.
> (*A Midsummer Night's Dream*, II. i.)

> How sweet the moonlight sleeps upon this bank!
> Here will we sit, and let the sounds of music
> Creep in our ears: soft stillness and the night
> Become the touches of sweet harmony.
> Sit, Jessica. Look, how the floor of heaven
> Is thick inlaid with patines of bright gold:
> There's not the smallest orb which thou behold'st

> But in his motion like an angel sings,
> Still quiring to the young-eyed cherubims,
> Such harmony is in immortal souls;
> But whilst this muddy vesture of decay
> Doth grossly close it in, we cannot hear it.
> (*The Merch*

OTHER PROBLEMS

Many speakers make the *S* predominate far m unnecessary increase in muscular pressure Both the tongue and the breathing may be ir impression of pushing or spitting the *S* ou Others frequently linger over these sounds as their sibilance. Leave should be taken of an When these sounds are correct, there is no their presence is already only too noticeable

MAINTAINING VOCAL TONE

Where vocal tone is concerned, consonan necessary evil. Necessary, because they a tone is articulated into speech, and evil managed, they interfere unduly with the tone, and not infrequently ruin it.

The consonants which should first with the resonator are those which cau and at the same time require the least exclude all voiceless consonants and all continuants *M*, *N*, and *L* are of speci may acquire the ability to move the lip ment of tone. To this end vowels ar most open position of the resonator of the tongue and lips respectively, vowel should be practised in associa at present we are more concerned w ciple than with its extension to all

Exercise 1

The conditions favourable to good this and all exercises incorporati erect poise; the deep, controlle

Exercise 4

For *L* the tongue tip articulation is the same as for *N*, but the soft palate is not lowered and the breath flows over the sides of the tongue, whilst the tongue tip is in approximation with the upper gums. This exercise is performed slowly at first, but the speed is gradually increased until extreme rapidity of tongue movement and clarity of formation are present in equal proportions. When this can be done, the exercise should be performed with equal rapidity in combination with *M* and *N*, although in the case of these consonants, it is first necessary to establish the tone before proceeding to rapidity. This rapid practice is extremely necessary, as through it we become conscious of the sense of touch possessed by the lips and tongue tip, and through this muscular consciousness we are able to focus the attention in the very fore-front of the mouth. This sensation of forward placing of the tone, and forward production of the articulation, is of paramount importance, since one of the distinguishing features of the well-managed voice is this very sensation that the whole act of speech is concerned solely with this area of the articulatory apparatus.

Exercise 5

The three consonants are then treated in the same way, one after the other using the vowel figure opposite, i.e.

MAHNAHLAH, MAYNAYLAY, MEENEELEE, MAYNAYLAY,

MAHNAHLAH, MAWNAWLAW, MOONOOLOO,

MAWNAWLAW, MAHNAHLAH.

Exercise 6

The vowels are then prefixed by *TH*, and then by *V* and *Z*.

Exercise 7

These six consonants are then practised one after the other without the insertion of a vowel –

M N L TH V Z

The tone is to be continuous throughout.

Exercise 8

Then in association with all the vowels and to different rhythms –

MÁH ŃAH ĹAH THAH VAH ZAH
MÁY ŃAY ĹAY THAY VAY ZAY
MÉE ŃEE ĹEE THEE VEE ZEE
MÁW ŃAW ĹAW THAW VAW ZAW
MÓO ŃOO ĹOO THOO VOO ZOO

The sound is to be continuous, thus –

MÓOŃOOĹOOTHOOVOOZOO

the spacing above being adopted for clarity.

Exercise 9

The rhythm is then altered and a great many changes may be rung,
e.g. –

MÄH ŇAH LAH ṪHAH V̆AH ŽAH
MÄH ŇAH LĂH ṪHAH V̆AH ŽAH

Exercise 10

The exercise is then made continuous and in this form is more difficult than it appears.

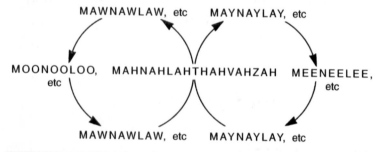

The genius of a language conditions its speech sounds. Though
the English language has perhaps more than its due share of
consonants, and a preponderance of sibilants owing to its grammatical structure, it is just these facts which give it its virility, and
this happens also to be a quality which is essential to true clarity
of articulation.

INTERPLAY OF VOWELS AND CONSONANTS

The interplay of vowels and their durational values, and the range of consonantal and syllabic variety, are nowhere better heard than in –

> Angels and ministers of grace defend us! –
> Be thou a spirit of health or goblin damn'd,
> Bring with thee airs from heaven or blasts from hell,
> Be thy intents wicked or charitable,
> Thou comest in such a questionable shape
> That I will speak to thee: I'll call thee Hamlet,
> King, father, royal Dane: O, answer me!
> Let me not burst in ignorance; but tell
> Why thy canonized bones, hearsed in death,
> Have burst their cerements; why the sepulchre,
> Wherein we saw thee quietly inurn'd,
> Hath oped his ponderous and marble jaws
> To cast thee up again!
>
> > (*Hamlet*, I. iv. – William Shakespeare.)

But to whom else should we look for wonders such as these?

AUDIBILITY

It is sometimes instructive to count the number of vowels and consonants occurring in a given passage. In Hamlet's opening speech to the Players from the beginning to the first full stop, the proportion is forty-two vowels to sixty-two consonants. And all in thirty-eight words! A nice indication of what must be done! More or less equal value must be given to tone and consonants with the emphasis, if anywhere, on the latter. In the whole speech, out of a total of one hundred and forty-four words, no fewer than eighty are terminated by a consonant. Conclusive proof of what is required of the consonants where audibility is concerned.

CONSONANTAL COMBINATIONS

Consider too the English way with plurals of words and the past tense. 'Task, tasks, tasked; clasp, clasps, clasped.' And its liking for doubling and even trebling consonantal beginnings; 'ripe, tripe, stripe.' And what of 'sprinkle'? Six consonants to one poor miserable vowel. But sufficient indication has been given of what is required of the actor where initial and final consonant groups are involved.

There follows a list of the simplest and most complicated consonantal endings and some tricky consonantal beginnings. A word of warning, however, must be added.

It has already been made clear that the production of vowel tone should be characterized by a complete absence of muscular force and tension in the resonators. The clarity of consonants, on the other hand, depends upon the muscular agility with which the tongue moves from one position to another, making all the adjustments with precision and accuracy. The clarity of the explosives depends upon the firmness of the contacts and the sharp release of the articulating organs. When a purely articulatory exercise is undertaken it is essential that the respective functions of the resonator and the articulators should not be confused. The tone must always be free and flowing and the energy with which the consonants are formed must never be allowed to spread to the production of tone. In these exercises the tone must always be produced legato, the staccato effect being confined to the consonants. The different action of the two instruments must never be confused if the tone is to remain unimpaired and freely produced on the breath, and this is the stage at which self-inculcation of these principles must begin.

Exercise 1

OOP OHP AWP AHP AYP EEP
OOB OHB AWB AHB AYB EEB

OOPT OHPT AWPT AHPT AYPT EEPT
OOSPT OHSPT AWSPT AHSPT AYSPT EESPT

Exercise 2

OOT OHT AWT AHT AYT EET
OOD OHD AWD AHD AYD EED

OOST OHST AWST AHST AYST EEST
OOZD OHZD AWZD AHZD AYZD EEZD

Exercise 3

OOSTS OHSTS AWSTS AHSTS AYSTS EESTS

Exercise 4

OOST STOO. OHST STOH. AWST STAW. AHST STAH.

AYST STAY. EEST STEE.

Exercise 5

OOK OHK AWK AHK AYK EEK
OOG OHG AWG AHG AYG EEG

OOKT OHKT AWKT AHKT AYKT EEKT
OOSKT OHSKT AWSKT AHSKT AYSKT EESKT

Exercise 6

OOKT TOO. OHKT TOH. AWKT TAW. AHKT TAH.

AYKT TAY. EEKT TEE.

Exercise 7

OOSKT TOO. OHSKT TOH. AWSKT TAW. AHSKT TAH.

AYSKT TAY. EESKT TEE.

Exercise 8

OOTH OHTH AWTH AHTH AYTH EETH
OOSTH OHSTH AWSTH AHSTH AYSTH EESTH

OOSTHS OHSTHS AWSTHS AHSTHS AYSTHS EESTHS
OOT,THS OHT,THS AWT,THS AHT,THS AYT,THS EET,THS

Exercise 9

OOST THOO. OHST THOH. AWST THAW. AHST THAH.
AYST THAY. EEST THEE.

Exercise 10

OOSTH TOO. OHSTH TOW. AWSTH TAW. AHSTH TAH.
AYSTH TAY. EESTH TEE.

Exercise 11

OOF OHF AWF AHF AYF EEF

OOV OHV AWV AHV AYV EEV

OOF,THS. OHF,THS. AWF,THS. AHF,THS. AYF,THS.
EEF,THS.

Exercise 12

OOV THOO. OHV THOH. AWV THAW. AHV THAH
AYV THAY. EEV THEE.

Exercise 13

OOM OHM AWM AHM AYM EEM

OON OHN AWN AHN AYN EEN

OONG OHNG AWNG AHNG AYNG EENG

Exercise 14

PLOO PLOH PLAW PLAH PLAY PLEE

BLOO BLOH BLAW BLAH BLAY BLEE

KLOO KLOH KLAW KLAH KLAY KLEE

GLOO GLOH GLAW GLAH GLAY GLEE

PROO PROH PRAW PRAH PRAY PREE

BROO BROH BRAW BRAH BRAY BREE

TROO TROH TRAW TRAH TRAY TREE

DROO DROH DRAW DRAH DRAY DREE

KROO KROH KRAW KRAH KRAY KREE

GROO GROH GRAW GRAH GRAY GREE

SPROO SPROH SPRAW SPRAH SPRAY SPREE

STROO STROH STRAW STRAH STRAY STREE

FROO FROH FRAW FRAH FRAY FREE

THROO THROH THRAW THRAH THRAY THREE

SHROO SHROH SHRAW SHRAH SHRAY SHREE

INTRUSIVE VOWELS

No vowel must be inserted between the pairs which prefix the vowels.

This intrusive vowel may be avoided by taking up the position for the second consonant during the closure for the first. Thus when *L* and *R* follow the explosives the tongue assumes the position for these sounds during the stop for the explosives. In 'troo' and 'droo,' the *T* is made further back than in 'too' to facilitate this method of articulation. This is, of course, the customary mode of procedure, so it is necessary for consideration to be given to such matters only by those who insert the *ER*.

MORE PRACTICE FOR THE LIPS AND TONGUE

Consonants in final positions, and those which are in groups, are those which cause the greatest difficulty and which are frequently omitted or inaudibly articulated, and for this reason they have been placed in final positions for practice. It is valuable to practise them in initial positions to stimulate the movement of the lips and tongue, thus –

ṔPPṔPPṔPP ṔAH ṔPPṔPPṔPP ṔAY ṔPPṔPPṔPP ṔEE, etc.

ḂBBḂBBḂBB ḂAH ḂBBḂBBḂBB ḂAY ḂBBḂBBḂBB ḂEE

ṪTTṪTTṪTT ṪAH ṪTTṪTTṪTT ṪAY ṪTTṪTTṪTT ṪEE, etc.

ḊDDḊDDḊDD ḊAH ḊDDḊDDḊDD ḊAY ḊDDḊDDḊDD ḊEE

ḰKKḰKKḰKK ḰAH ḰKKḰKKḰKK ḰAY ḰKKḰKKḰKK ḰEE, etc.

ǴGGǴGGǴGG ǴAH ǴGGǴGGǴGG ǴAY ǴGGǴGGǴGG ǴEE

each consonant representing a separate articulation.

SILENT EXERCISES

The tongue and lips may be exercised silently in the following way.

Exercise 1

Alternately point and spread the tongue to a rhythmic count. In the pointed position the tip should be protruded, and in the spread position the tongue should lie just behind, and midway between, the upper and lower teeth.

Exercise 2
Funnel the tongue so that its edges curl up at the sides. Alternate this with *AH*.

Exercise 3
Try to touch the nose, and then the chin, with the tongue-tip alternately and in time.

Exercise 4
Roll the upper lip until it touches the nose. Roll the lower lip until it touches the chin.

Exercise 5
Without spreading the lips, but with vigorous rounding, pass rapidly through these vowel positions –

EE ÓO EE ŏŏ EE ÓH EE ÁW EE ǒ EE AH
OO ú EŔ OO á OO é OO ÁY OO ǐ OO EÉ.

EXERCISES WITH THE SHORT VOWELS
The so-called short vowels are often found in combination with a consonant and following *L*. There is seldom any difficulty in this articulation except when the *L* is faulty in formation, but exercises on them are included as it is better to err on the side of inclusion than omission where the consonants are concerned.

ŏŏNL ŏNL ŭNL ĕNL ăNL ĭNL
ŏŏNTL ŏNTL ŭNTL ĕNTL ăNTL ĭNTL
ŏŏNDL ŏNDL ŭNDL ĕNDL ăNDL ĭNDL
ŏŏMBL ŏMBL ŭMBL ĕMBL ăMBL ĭMBL
ŏŏPL ŏPL ŭPL ĕPL ăPL ĭPL
ŏŏBL ŏBL ŭBL ĕBL ăBL ĭBL
ŏŏSL ŏSL ŭSL ĕSL ăSL ĭSL
ŏŏFL ŏFL ŭFL ĕFL ăFL ĭFL

In all these cases the *L* is what is termed syllabic, which means that it forms a syllable without the assistance of a vowel.

FURTHER PRACTICE MATERIAL
Many of these consonantal combinations and some new ones will
be found in the following –

> Reason thus with life –
> If I do lose thee, l do lose a thing
> That none but fools would keep: a breath thou art,
> Servile to all the skyey influences
> That do this habitation, where thou keep'st,
> Hourly affflict: merely, thou art death's fool;
> For him thou labour'st by thy flight to shun,
> And yet runn'st toward him still. Thou art not noble;
> For all th' accommodations that thou bear'st
> Are nursed by baseness. Thou'rt by no means valiant;
> For thou dost fear the soft and tender fork
> Of a poor worm. Thy best of rest is sleep,
> And that thou oft provok'st; yet grossly fear'st
> Thy death, which is no more. Thou art not thyself;
> For thou exist'st on many thousand grains
> That issue out of dust. Happy thou art not;
> For what thou hast not, still thou striv'st to get,
> And what thou hast, forget'st. Thou art not certain;
> For thy complexion shifts to strange effects,
> After the moon.
> (*Measure for Measure*, III. i – William Shakespeare.)

Certainly a full measure of consonants!

'The greatest story of past times' was the unanimous verdict of
the critic's circle when they were asked to *Arctic Snows*, the latest
documentary to be revived this year. The strength of six-sixths of
this starkest drama consists simply of the close-ups of the snow-
covered clothes, the choicest shots, and the swiftness with which
the climax is built up. Fast-moving down to the last cue, with a
series of swift strokes, the climax seems to burst before our aston-
ished sight. The width and breadth of the conception is striking.
Smith's slick sixth scene is most moving when, past caring, he
hacks through the snows with the strength of hardest steel to
rescue his companions, who look like ghosts seen through the

Arctic mists. The seventh scene of this breathless epic is past
description. The snows cease, the mists clear, and as the party
prepare for their last tasks, we see the screen flecked with choicest
stars.

Since this distressing tendency to sibilance in my speech seems
most certainly to constitute a serious set-back to my prospects of
success on the stage, l have, of necessity, enlisted the assistance of
this series of sentences, not essentially sensible, but so composed
as to exercise to the utmost those speech organs responsible for
producing (eventually I trust with some measure of success) this
troublesome sound. For I must confess, at present, l find myself
at a distinct disadvantage, since the splendid pathos and soul-
stirring sadness of my most emotional passages is simply shat-
tered by this distressing, distracting, whistling 'S,' which is
sufficient to give the least discerning audiences the impression
that they are listening to the hysterical hissing of incensed geese!

The practice of consonants brings home the fact, even more clearly
than in the case of the vowels, that speech is movement, and that
utterance consists of tone on which these movements are superimposed. That this is so, is borne out by our ability to make ourselves
understood by means of consonantal movement alone when this is
allied to the breath. Thus if any of the above lines are whispered,
with no attempt to make the words carry to an abnormal distance,
the element of tone is obviously non-existent, and yet what is said
is made intelligible by the movements of the articulatory organs.
The movements for the consonants are perhaps of more importance than those for the vowels in this respect.

GENERAL EXERCISES FOR BREATH, NOTE, TONE AND WORD
At this stage we are in a position where we may link the four factors
of breath, note, tone, and word together.

As before, the centre note may be alternately advanced and
lowered a semi-tone with the precautions to which reference has
already been made.

It is not necessary to confine oneself to scales. Simple easy
melodies, well within the compass of the voice, and preferably those
which do not demand the singing of *very* marked intervals, may be

most usefully employed. The main vowels should be taken first, and they should be prefixed by *H*. Each note of the melody is to be made distinct, and the voice is not to slide up to the note above or down to the note below that which is being sung. Next sing the whole tune on *M* and then on *N*, and then on *M, N, L*, plus any of the main vowels, and then on any consonant, first voiced and then voiceless, in combination with any of the vowels, and finally with the words of the chosen song.

Starting on a note at least a fourth below the top note of the compass, sing down the scale until a note one octave below is reached. On each note of the scale the first eight vowels of the previous exercise are to be sung prefixed first by *M* and then by *N* and, finally, by *L*.

This exercise is to be carried out with great rapidity and with light, agile movements of the lips and tongue.

Starting on a note at least a fourth above the lowest note of the compass, sing up in fourths until one octave above is reached.

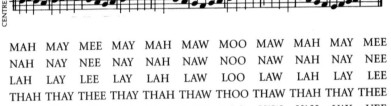

MAH	MAY	MEE	MAY	MAH	MAW	MOO	MAW	MAH	MAY	MEE
NAH	NAY	NEE	NAY	NAH	NAW	NOO	NAW	NAH	NAY	NEE
LAH	LAY	LEE	LAY	LAH	LAW	LOO	LAW	LAH	LAY	LEE
THAH	THAY	THEE	THAY	THAH	THAW	THOO	THAW	THAH	THAY	THEE
VAH	VAY	VEE	VAY	VAH	VAW	VOO	VAW	VAH	VAY	VEE
ZAH	ZAY	ZEE	ZAY	ZAH	ZAW	ZOO	ZAW	ZAH	ZAY	ZEE
THAH	THAY	THEE	THAY	THAH	THAW	THOO	THAW	THAH	THAY	THEE
FAH	FAY	FEE	FAY	FAH	FAW	FOO	FAW	FAH	FAY	FEE
SAH	SAY	SEE	SAY	SAH	SAW	SOO	SAW	SAH	SAY	SEE
PAH	PAY	PEE	PAY	PAH	PAW	POO	PAW	PAH	PAY	PEE
BAH	BAY	BEE	BAY	BAH	BAW	BOO	BAW	BAH	BAY	BEE
TAH	TAY	TEE	TAY	TAH	TAW	TOO	TAW	TAH	TAY	TEE
DAH	DAY	DEE	DAY	DAH	DAW	DOO	DAW	DAH	DAY	DEE
KAH	KAY	KEE	KAY	KAH	KAW	KOO	KAW	KAH	KAY	KEE
GAH	GAY	GEE	GAY	GAH	GAW	GOO	GAW	GAH	GAY	GEE

MAH	MAY	MEE	MAY	MAH	MAW	MOO	MAW	MAH
NAH	NAY	NEE	NAY	NAH	NAW	NOO	NAW	NAH
LAH	LAY	LEE	LAY	LAH	LAW	LOO	LAW	LAH
THAH	THAY	THEE	THAY	THAH	THAW	THOO	THAW	THAH
VAH	VAY	VEE	VAY	VAH	VAW	VOO	VAW	VAH
ZAH	ZAY	ZEE	ZAY	ZAH	ZAW	ZOO	ZAW	ZAH
THAH	THAY	THEE	THAY	THAH	THAW	THOO	THAW	THAH
FAH	FAY	FEE	FAY	FAH	FAW	FOO	FAW	FAH
SAH	SAY	SEE	SAY	SAH	SAW	SOO	SAW	SAH
PAH	PAY	PEE	PAY	PAH	PAW	POO	PAW	PAH
BAH	BAY	BEE	BAY	BAH	BAW	BOO	BAW	BAH
TAH	TAY	TEE	TAY	TAH	TAW	TOO	TAW	TAH
DAH	DAY	DEE	DAY	DAH	DAW	DOO	DAW	DAH
KAH	KAY	KEE	KAY	KAH	KAW	KOO	KAW	KAH
GAH	GAY	GEE	GAY	GAH	GAW	GOO	GAW	GAH

MAH MAY MEE MAY MAH MAW MOO MAW MAH MAY MEE MAY MAH MAW MOO MAW MAH
NAH NAY NEE NAY NAH NAW NOO NAW NAH NAY NEE NAY NAH NAW NOO NAW NAH
LAH LAY LEE LAY LAH LAW LOO LAW LAH LAY LEE LAY LAH LAW LOO LAW LAH
THAH THAY THEE THAY THAH THAW THOO THAW THAH THAY THEE THAY THAH THAW THOO THAW THAH
VAH VAY VEE VAY VAH VAW VOO VAW VAH VAY VEE VAY VAH VAW VOO VAW VAH
ZAH ZAY ZEE ZAY ZAH ZAW ZOO ZAW ZAH ZAY ZEE ZAY ZAH ZAW ZOO ZAW ZAH
THAH THAY THEE THAY THAH THAW THOO THAW THAH THAY THEE THAY THAH THAW THOO THAW THAH
FAH FAY FEE FAY FAH FAW FOO FAW FAH FAY FEE FAY FAH FAW FOO FAW FAH
SAH SAY SEE SAY SAH SAW SOO SAW SAH SAY SEE SAY SAH SAW SOO SAW SAH
PAH PAY PEE PAY PAH PAW POO PAW PAH PAY PEE PAY PAH PAW POO PAW PAH
BAH BAY BEE BAY BAH BAW BOO BAW BAH BAY BEE BAY BAH BAW BOO BAW BAHTAH TAY TEE
TAY TAH TAW TOO TAW TAH TAY TEE TAY TAH TAW TOO TAW TAH
DAH DAY DEE DAY DAH DAW DOO DAW DAH DAY DEE DAY DAH DAW DOO DAW DAh
KAH KAY KEE KAY KAH KAW KOO KAW KAH KAY KEE KAY KAH KAW KOO KAW KAH
GAH GAY GEE GAY GAH GAW GOO GAW GAH GAY GEE GAY GAH GAW GOO GAW GAH

This is to be done on a good, forward, resonant *M*. When the note an octave above the starting place is reached, the *M* is to be held for a second or two so that a ringing quality is felt strongly on the lips. They should then be opened on to an *AH*, which, prefixed by *M*, is to be sung staccato on each note down the scale until the starting point is reached. This exercise is valuable in helping to obtain clarity and firmness of attack. It should be continuous, with no break between the sections.

The following speeches provide demanding exercise for breath, note, tone and articulation of consonants.

Truewit. If you appear learned to an ignorant wench, or jocund to a sad, or witty to a foolish, why she presently begins to mistrust herself. You must approach them in their own height, their own line; for the contrary makes many, that fear to commit themselves to noble and worthy fellows, run into the embraces of a rascal. If she love wit, give verses, though you borrow them of a friend, or buy them, to have good. If valour, talk of your sword, and be frequent in the mention of quarrels, though you be staunch in fighting. If activity, be seen on your barbary often, or leaping over stools, for the credit of your back. If she love good clothes or dressing, have your learned council about you every morning, your French tailor, barber, linener, etc. Let your powder, your glass, and your comb be your dearest acquaintance. Take more care for the ornament of your head than the safety; and wish the commonwealth rather troubled, than a hair about you. That will take her. Then if she be covetous and craving, do you promise anything, and perform sparingly; so shall you keep her in appetite still. Seem as you would give, but be like a barren field, that yields little; or unlucky dice to foolish and hoping gamesters.

(*The Silent Woman* – Ben Jonson.)

Mistress Otter. By my integrity, I'll send you over to the Bankside; I'll commit you to the master of the Garden, if I hear but a syllable more. Must my house or my roof be polluted with the scent of bears and bulls, when it is perfumed for great ladies? Is this according to the instrument when I married you? that I would be princess, and reign in mine own house; and you would be my subject, and obey me? What did you bring me, should make you thus peremptory? do I allow you your half-crown a day, to spend where you will, among your gamesters, to vex and torment me at such times as these? Who gives you your maintenance, I pray you? who allows you your horse-meat and man's meat? your three pairs of apparel a year? your four pairs of stockings, one silk, three worsted? your clean linen, your bands and cuffs, when I can get you to wear them? – 'tis marle you have on them now. – Who graces you with courtiers or great personages, to speak to you out of their coaches, and come home to your house? Were you ever so much as look'd upon by a lord or a lady, before I married you, but on the Easter or Whitsun holidays? and then out of the banqueting-house window, when Ned Whiting or George Stone were at the stake?

(*The Silent Woman* – Ben Jonson.)

How this vile world is changed! in former days
Prologues were serious speeches before plays;
Grave solemn things, as graces are to feasts,
Where poets begged a blessing from their guests.
But now, no more like suppliants we come;
A Play makes war, and Prologue is the drum:
Armed with keen satire, and with pointed wit,
We threaten you who do for judges sit,
To save our plays, or else we'll damn your pit.
But for your comfort, it falls out to-day,
We've a young author, and his first-born play;
So, standing only on his good behaviour,
He's very civil, and entreats your favour.
Not but the man has malice, would he show it,
But, on my conscience, he's a bashful poet;
You think that strange – no matter, he'll outgrow it.
Well, I'm his advocate – by me he prays you,
(I don't know whether I shall speak to please you)
He prays – O bless me what shall I do now!
Hang me, if I know what he prays, or how!
And 'twas the prettiest Prologue as he wrote it!
Well, the deuce take me, if I ha'n't forgot it!
O Lord, for Heaven's sake excuse the Play,
Because, you know, if it be damned to-day,
I shall be hanged for wanting what to say.

For my sake then – but I'm in such confusion,
I cannot stay to hear your resolution.

(Runs off)

(Prologue (spoken by Mrs. Bracegirdle) to *The Old Bachelor* –
William Congreve.)

Of those few fools who with ill stars are curst,
Sure scribbling fools, called poets, fare the worst:
For they're a sort of fools which Fortune makes,
And after she has made 'em fools, forsakes.
With Nature's oafs 'tis quite a different case,
For Fortune favours all her idiot-race.
In her own nest the cockoo-eggs we find,
O'er which she broods to hatch the changeling-kind.
No portion for her own she has to spare,
So much she dotes on her adopted care.

   Poets are bubbles, by the town drawn in,
Suffered at first some trifling stakes to win;
But what unequal hazards do they run!
Each time they write they venture all they've won:
The squire that's buttered still, is sure to be undone.
This author heretofore has found your favour;
But pleads no merit from his past behaviour.
To build on that might prove a vain presumption,
Should grants, to poets made, admit resumption:
And in Parnassus he must lose his seat,
If that be found a forfeited estate.

   He owns with toil he wrought the following scenes;
But, if they're naught, ne'er spare him for his pains:
Damn him the more; have no commiseration
For dullness on mature deliberation,
He swears he'll not resent one hissed-off scene,
Nor, like those peevish wits, his play maintain,
Who, to assert their sense, your taste arraign.
Some plot we think he has, and some new thought;
Some humour too, no farce; but that's a fault.
Satire, he thinks, you ought not to expect;
For so reformed a town who dares correct?

To please, this time, has been his sole pretence,
He'll not instruct, lest it should give offence.
Should he by chance a knave or fool expose,
That hurts none here, sure here are none of those:
In short, our play shall (with your leave to show it)
Give you one instance of a passive poet,
Who to your judgments yields all resignation;
So save or damn, after your own discretion.

(Prologue (spoken by Mr. Betterton) to *The Way of the World* – William Congreve.)

6 • THE VOICE IN ACTION

In the opening chapters a distinction was drawn between voice and speech. It was remarked that the voice was, at one and the same time, a tone-producing instrument, and a word-producing instrument. Both tone and word, as we have seen, are referable to the resonator. Tone, it is true, cannot exist without the element of note, but tone is imparted to the note solely by the cavities through which it passes. The tone of the voice must therefore of necessity possess not only general character but also specific character, since the resonator must assume a certain shape, and, as we already know, shape is responsible for the vowel which is heard. In addition, the resonator may be closed, either partially or completely, in the formation of the consonants. It is these movements, for shaping the vowels and articulating the consonants, which are impressed on the tone. The resonator therefore has a musical function in producing tone, and a linguistic function in assuming the shapes for the vowels and carrying out the movements necessary to form the consonants. That this distinction is not merely theoretical may be borne out in practice.

SECURING CLEAR ARTICULATION

Exercise 1
To this end the following lines are to be spoken in the whispered voice. Full attention is to be paid to the neatness and clarity of the articulation, and the consonant movements are to be felt far forward in the front of the mouth. The use of the word 'felt' is not fortuitous. The sense of touch possessed by the tongue-tip and the lips is to be fully utilized. This, combined with the feeling of freedom as the breath passes through the unrestricted resonator, leads to the impression that the act of speech is concerned with the very forefront of the mouth and with that area alone.

Ah, Moon of my Delight who know'st no Wane,
The Moon of Heaven is rising once again:
How oft hereafter rising shall she look
Through this same garden after me – in vain!

I sometimes think that never blows so red
The Rose as where some buried Ceasar bled;
That every Hyacinth the Garden wears
Dropt in her Lap from some once lovely Head.

And this reviving Herb whose tender Green
Fledges the River-Lip on which we lean –
Ah, lean upon it lightly! for who knows
From what once lovely Lip it springs unseen!

(Fitzgerald.)

These three stanzas contain no fewer than one hundred and ninety-two consonant sounds and, of these, only eleven involve the back of the tongue. The lips and tongue tip, therefore, make one hundred and eighty-two separate articulations in the course of speaking twelve lines! It is no wonder that clarity depends upon the precision and forwardness of the movements involved.

Exercise 2
The lines are then repeated one by one, only this time they are to be intoned. The tone is to be full and aesthetically satisfying, and clear and bright, so that every vowel sounds as if it were being made as far forward as possible. In combining tone and movement in this way, we are conscious only of the extremities of the instrument. We direct the breath so that it comes from the bases of the lungs with firm, even pressure, and we shape and mould the tone by the energy and precision of the articulatory movement, but if the ability to speak with the open throat has been achieved there should be no consciousness of the mechanisms involved in the production of note and tone.

THE TECHNIQUE OF INFLECTION
When this can be done, and the principle is clearly grasped, it is but one stage further to give the note its freedom, so that it responds to the intention of the author and speaker, and 'points' the meaning by inflectional variety. Comparatively little inflection is called for in this passage. Immediately character and complex situations are present the issue becomes confused, because the mind is apt to become divided between the character and the technique by which it is portrayed. For the present the alliance between tone and move-

ment must not only be grasped, but sensed bodily, although ultimately the reverse situation obtains. The actor, once the method has become incorporated in his or her technique, is completely unconcerned with the voice as such, which responds automatically to the demands made upon it.

Exercise 3

Black is the beauty of the brightest day;
The golden ball of heaven's eternal fire,
That danc'd with glory on the silver waves,
Now wants the fuel that inflam'd his beams;
And all with faintness, and for foul disgrace,
He binds his temple with a frowning cloud,
Ready to darken earth with endless night.
Zenocrate, that gave him light and life,
Whose eyes shot fire from their ivory brows,
And temper'd every soul with lively heat,
Now by the malice of the angry skies,
Whose jealousy admits no second mate,
Draws in the comfort of her latest breath,
All dazzled with the hellish mists of death.

(Tamburlaine, II. iv.)

The single moulded lines and the forward impetus of Marlowe's verse make the passage singularly applicable to the methods advocated. The whole scene is a perfect example of what is demanded of the voice by romantic tragedy at this stage of its development.

Exercise 4

Elizabethan drama, being predominantly masculine, does not provide an equally good example for women. If desired the following lines from *Comus* may be substituted for Marlowe's verses.

The Star that bids the Shepherd fold,
Now the top of Heav'n doth hold,
And the gilded Car of Day,
His glowing Axle doth allay
In the steep Atlantick stream,
And the slope Sun his upward beam

Shoots against the dusky Pole,
Pacing toward the other gole
Of his Chamber in the East.
Mean while welcom Joy, and Feast,
Midnight shout, and revelry,
Tipsie dance, and Jollity.
Braid your Locks with rosie Twine
Dropping odours, dropping Wine.
Rigor now is gon to bed,
And Advice with scrupulous head,
Strict Age, and sowre Severity,
With their grave Saws in slumber ly.
We that are of purer fire
Imitate the Starry Quire,
Who in their nightly watchfull Sphears,
Lead in swift round the Months and Years.
The Sounds, and Seas with all their finny drove
Now to the moon in wavering Morrice move.
And on the Tawny Sands and Shelves,
Trip the pert Fairies and the dapper Elves;
By dimpled Brook, and Fountain brim,
The Wood-Nymphs deckt with Daisies trim,
Their merry wakes and pastimes keep:
What hath night to do with sleep?
Night hath better sweets to prove,
Venus now wakes, and wak'ns Love....
Com, knit hands, and beat the ground,
In a light fantastick round.

(*Comus* – John Milton.)

Exercise 5

O God! methinks it were a happy life,
To be no better than a homely swain;
To sit upon a hill, as I do now,
To carve out dials quaintly, point by point,
Thereby to see the minutes how they run,
How many makes the hour full complete;
How many hours bring about the day;
How many days will finish up the year;
How many years a mortal man may live.

When this is known, then to divide the times: –
So many hours must I tend my flock;
So many hours must I take my rest;
So many hours must I contemplate;
So many hours must I sport myself;
So many days my ewes have been with young;
So many weeks ere the poor fools will ean;
So many months ere I shall shear the fleece:
So minutes, hours, days, months and years,
Past over to the end they were created,
Would bring white hairs unto a quiet grave.
Ah, what a life were this! how sweet! how lovely!

(*Henry VI*, III. ii. v.)

Exercise 6

And just as Shakespeare himself progressed from this stage to the
intricacies of the sleepless *Henry IV*, and the imprisoned *Richard II*,
so the speaker must first master the rudimentary yet fundamental
vocal principles involved.

Alas, she hath from France too long been chased!
And all her husbandry doth lie on heaps,
Corrupting in its own fertility.
Her vine, the merry cheerer of the heart,
Unpruned dies; her hedges even-pleacht,
Like prisoners wildly overgrown with hair,
Put forth disorder'd twigs; her fallow leas
The darnel, hemlock, and rank fumitory,
Do root upon, while that the coulter rusts,
That should deracinate such savagery;
The even mead, that erst brought sweetly forth
The freckled cowslip, burnet, and green clover,
Wanting the scythe, all uncorrected, rank,
Conceives by idleness, and nothing teems
But hateful docks, rough thistles, kecksies, burs,
Losing both beauty and utility.

(*Henry V*, V. ii.)

Women may substitute Titania's lines

These are the forgeries of jealousy:
And never, since the middle summer's spring,
Met we on hill, in dale, forest, or mead,
By paved mountain or by rushy brook,
Or in the beached margent of the sea,
To dance our ringlets to the whistling wind,
But with thy brawls thou hast disturbed our sport.
Therefore the winds, piping to us in vain,
As in revenge, have sucked up from the sea
Contagious fogs; which, falling in the land,
Hath every pelting river made so proud,
That they have overborne their continents.
The ox hath therefore stretched his yoke in vain,
The plowman lost his sweat, and the green corn
Hath rotted ere his youth attained a beard;
The fold stands empty in the drowned field,
And crows are fatted with the murrion flock,
The nine men's morris is filled up with mud;
And the quaint mazes in the wanton green,
For lack of tread, are undistinguishable.
The human mortals want their winter here;
No night is now with hymn or carol blest.
Therefore the moon, the governess of the floods,
Pale in her anger, washes all the air,
That rheumatic diseases do abound.
And thorough this distemperature we see
The seasons alter: hoary-headed frosts
Fall in the fresh lap of the crimson rose,
And on old Hiem's thin and icy crown
An odorous chaplet of sweet summer buds
Is, in mockery, set. The spring, the summer,
The childing autumn, angry winter, change
Their wonted liveries; and the mazed world,
By their increase, now knows not which is which.
And this same progeny of evils comes
From our debate, from our dissension;
We are their parents and original.

(*Midsummer Night's Dream*, II., i.)

The process is here more complex, and is conveyed by a series of visual images in broken phrases of varied length.

These examples are all taken from romantic plays in verse, not only because the highest demands on the voice are made by such plays, but also because they in themselves often call forth the best that is in a voice. The intention, of course, is not that everything which is spoken should be subjected to the same vocal treatment in the matter of tone. If this were so, it would be the negation of technique. It is a simple matter to give a lighter character to the tone when occasion demands, but richness of texture can never be suddenly acquired. The process takes time, and the technique is built up gradually.

SOUND AND MEANING

We can now return once more to the nature of the medium in which the actor works. It is seen to be not only sound, but sound which is meaning, and meaning which is sound. The sound is tone, which embodies and shows forth the emotional conception of a role. At the same time, this variable tone, variable in volume, in pitch and texture, carries the movements of speech to a distance. The movements give definition to the tone and therefore to the emotions of the character. The movements themselves must be clear-cut and firm, and in the very forefront of the mouth.

FORMATION OF VOWELS

Up to this point, utterance has been approached from the musical angle alone. We have considered to what extent we may arrive at perfection by a conscious direction of the movements of our voice mechanism on correct physiological lines. Such adaptation as is necessary has been governed by the extent to which the normal action of the organs will allow of adaptation as determined by the physical laws governing the production of sound. This is the vital standard to which it is essential to adhere; the standard by which alone the latent beauties and inherent qualities of the voice may be not only revealed but preserved. Such matters are removed from controversy, resting as they do upon perfection of utterance, achieved through the movement of living organs working in co-ordinated harmony in the service of an art. In the descriptions, certain variations are noted for those who may need to acquire a dialect.

SIMPLE VOWELS

The following examples offer the opportunity for that iteration of movement which is essential when the adoption of a new habit is necessary. If a vowel is deemed incorrect, it is only the frequent repetition of the newly-acquired position, under the control of the sense of hearing, which will ensure the incorporation of the correct sound.

Exercise for *OO*

The vowel in 'loose', 'true', 'through' [uː]. This is frequently incorrectly diphthongized so that *ŏo* + *OO* [uuː] or *OO* + *W* [uw] result. The tongue and lips must assume the correct position at the outset, and must not creep up to the position. Marked dialectal pronunciation occurs when the resonance is too high, as in Cockney when the tongue is too advanced. The correct position may be obtained by whistling a low note.

> There is much ado about the new roof show, *Moonlight in Peru*, due in June at Boosey's Jubilee Rooms. Juan de la Rue has imbued the show with the magic of Peruvian tunes. The show includes the Two Loons in Human Roulette, The Crooning Goose, The Blue Lupin Troupe of hoola-hoola cuties in their cunning cutaways who ululate their roulades with bravura, the Human Jewels, and the Broody Booths with their Boomerang in Buhl. As an alluring bonne-bouche the show concludes with Cerulean Mood, in which beauteous, blooming Cubans croon in coloratura to a ground tune of bassoons.

Exercise for *o͝o*

The vowel in 'cushion', 'could', 'wood' [u]. There are no marked varieties of this vowel. Especial care must be taken to round the lips adequately and to avoid undue influence by a following *L*. The careless, colloquial, unrounded *o͝o* in 'good-bye' must be avoided.

> Cook said good-bye to her pudding-basins and cookery books when she took her bosom friend, Miss Goodchild, to Fulham to see Wolsey Foote in *The Hook-Nosed Crook*. The fulsome and ebullient Foote had fulfilled his wish to put Pushkin aside for good. Putting the stolen bullion in a bushel basket hooked from the butcher, he conceals it in some bushes at the foot of a cul-de-sac at Goodwood. But Fullwood, the bushy-bearded footman,

hooded in worsted, was a looker-on. Protected by a holster full of bullets, he loses his foothold in the bulrushes by a brook, skilfully covering his splashes by imitating the cuckoo. When the crook forsook the bushes, Fullwood took the bullion and put crowsfoot in its place. All this we heard from cook as she took a last look round the kitchen before saying good-night.

Exercise for *OH*
The vowel in 'though', 'show', 'home' [əu]. Although *OH* is included in the list of simple vowels on the Resonator Scale, it must be noted that it is truly a diphthong. The most usual pronunciation of this sound begins with the neutral sound [ə] as its first element and the tongue rises, as the lips round, towards o͞o for the second element. A 'pure' or single sound is frequently used by Scottish and northern speakers. The *OH* sound is subject to many variations among speakers; sometimes starting too near ŭ, or too near ŏ.

Rosario, the Polish mezzo-soprano, broke her fast with hot chocolate and toasted rolls in her state-room on board the *Ocean Queen*. Interviewed by a host of reporters, she was seen against a background of mauve and snow white gladioli, gazing out of a porthole, and alternately toying with a rope of pearls with her beautifully moulded hands and smoking a cigarette in an outsize golden holder. Known at home to the beaumonde for her extensive wardrobe she is happiest when in homespun and brogues she hoes among her roses and potatoes. To billposters she is the most photographed mezzo known. In October and November she will be heard at the Rotunda in her favourite role of Mimi which she has made her very own. Ultimately she broke the silence in controlled and hollow tones. "I only hope London will like my Mimi." She rose with unceremonious and irreproachable composure as with a roguish, provoking smile she autographed an endless number of photographs.

Exercise for *AW*
The vowel in 'law', 'corn', 'caught' [ɔː]. Peculiarly liable to 'throaty' pronunciation as a result of tension at the base of the tongue. The lip rounding must not be extreme, otherwise a type of *AW*, resembling *OH*, will result. This may often be heard from London dialect speakers in whom 'saw' and 'door' become 'sohwer' and 'dohwer.'

Northern and Scottish speakers who wish to acquire the southern pronunciation must take considerable care when this sound is followed by an *R* in the spelling. In the example given all the *AW* sounds are identical in southern English.

An enormous audience foregathered at the Forum for the first night of Yorkshire Dawn. A mawkish, maudlin play, which stands or falls by the awe of Lord Cawth in act four when, torn on the horns of a dilemma, he pauses before four doors, before greeting the aforesaid Yorkshire Dawn on the lawn. The distinguished company were not at all well served by George their director, a staunch believer in the drawn out pause and the theory of the fourth wall. They were forced to talk upstage, which caused them all to be almost inaudible. The author in taking his curtain call was given a raw deal. Torn between the plaudits of the pit and the appalling cat calls of the gallery, he addressed himself in a short, plausible speech to his supporters in the stalls, by whom he was greeted with a roar of applause.

Exercise for ŏ
The vowel in 'off,' 'cough,' 'long' [ɑ]. The principal variation in the formation of this sound is the failure to round the lips sufficiently, in which case it becomes a type of *AH*. This is characteristic of some American speech. 'Solve,' 'revolve,' etc., must be pronounced with ŏ and not with *OH*.

It is not often I receive such a shock as I got when not long ago I read in the popular gossip columns that the populace will shortly be offered all the horrors of the Roman Colosseum. It appears that the popularity of dog racing has worn off. The dogs have had their very long day and have lost their monopoly. It will no longer be possible to say with jocularity that Dad has gone to the dogs. Pater has gone to the lions will be heard more often as time goes on. This offers great possibilities for obstreperous officers and ostracized tax collectors and any others numbered among the great unwanted. Such could make their swan-song by offering themselves to the lions and thus reconquer their lost popularity with the population. This is not contemplated as yet, for atomically-operated robots will be used. Concealed vox humana organ pipes will be operated softly to croon the spectators to their boxes. Not long afterwards the arena will throb realistically with the victims' simulated sobs.

Exercise for *AH*

The vowel in 'calm,' 'hard,' 'past' [ɑː]. Peculiarly liable to 'throaty' pronunciation through tensing the base of the tongue, in which case the pronunciation becomes 'dark' and AW-like. Great care must be taken not to allow the tongue to assume a 'fronted' dialectal pronunciation, a feature of the speech of some Londoners, and characteristic of Australians and New Zealanders.

'Carlotta's Past.' To be released at last in March, this epic drama completely surpasses the earlier silent version. Arthur Marks plans to co-star Martha Marr and Charlie Garth. A glance at the scenario in advance was given me by Arthur in his smart apartment overlooking Marble Arch. Startling and remarkable transformations have been made. It was felt that Carlotta's passing aberrations would be laughable to-day, and would give little chance for all the present refinements of cinema art. The last episode, in the earlier version, depicted Carlotta prancing as Margaret of Navarre at the Arts Dance. Now we are transported to Alexandria, where we glance at Martha held captive by Charles, who plays the Pasha, and runs a smart line in harems in a side street off a bazaar. Carlotta, half clad in scarlet, reflected in the water of a marble bath fanned by slaves with palms, is commanded to dance a nautch dance under the dark eyes of the Pasha. She salaams with mask-like charm and dances to the strains of muted guitars, played adagio from afar.

Exercise for *ŭ*

The vowel in 'one,' 'young,' 'bun' [ʌ] . This is often given too high a resonant pitch with the result that the vowel sounds too like a short 'fronted' *AH*. Northern speakers will possibly need to acquire this sound, as it may not be in their repertoire at all. In broad Yorkshire, for example, the *o͞o* vowel is substituted and, in other cases, a vowel lying between *o͞o* and *ŭ*. Special care is necessary when *u* is followed by *L*; 'bulb,' for example, must not become 'bolb.'

The youngest inhabitants of Humpton-cum-Dunton summed up last Monday as the dullest they had ever suffered. Summoned by a fanfare of trumpets from the turrets of Humpton Hall they made their way to the sunken garden to witness a performance of the Dumb Brothers organized by Lady Lumley in aid of Our Young Friends Fund. Unluckily the summer sun was true to form and everyone put his umbrella up when a rumble of thunder announced the rain which came down in bucketfuls. The youngest and humblest thus saw the play through an utter forest of umbrella handles. The advent of the thunder was hailed by Lady Lumley as a lovely and consummate effect as it heralded the scene in which the somewhat dumb brother is struck by the utterly dumb brother whilst culling buttercups. The somewhat dumb brother then becomes utterly dumb, so giving rise to the title. The humbler inhabitants of Humpton were also struck dumb by the glumness of the whole proceedings as, one by one, they trudged through the mud to the Dun Cow, to their tea of butterless buns and honey. 'Some fun,' they muttered, one and all, looking somewhat glum.

Exercise for *ER*

The vowel in 'heard,' 'nurse,' 'verse,' 'myrrh' [əː]. The principal variations in this vowel occur with speakers who pronounce the *R* in some form. When the *R* is not pronounced, care must be taken not to give this vowel too 'forward' a position in which case the tongue approaches ĕ ('then').

The curtain rises to disclose to the retina a circular room furnished with all the appurtenances of modern comfort. A circular table placed centre is covered with purple serge and supports an epergne surmounted by odoriferous lavender, and a box encrusted with seed pearls. Down centre, on a firm base, is set a pedestal surmounted by the figure of Napoleon. A sofa and thirteen chairs are observed supporting the walls. The rest of the stage is perfectly clear for the actors' turns. A clock strikes thirteen. The reverberations die away, and through the open door up centre, framing a parterre of wallflowers, enters Sir Ferdinand. His face is stern. His words are terse. His nerves are worse. He speaks in verse.

Exercise for ă
The vowel in 'glad,' 'plait' [æ]. Care must be taken to avoid a pinched, affected pronunciation approximating to ĕ, or too open a position, which is characteristic of Midland and Northern speech. Do not spread the lips.

On the strand at Clacton, a band of fascinated graphic artists gathered round Professor Bangham, who demonstrated the theatrical value of plastics. To the garrulent professor, who held that the theatre lacked plasticity, canvas flats were anathema. With dramatic hands, he amassed and scattered sap green and gamboge plastic on the sand. With a flash of the hand he simulated the lapping of wavelets against an imaginary crag. 'What a saving in time when no canvas has to be dabbed and splashed with paint.' With emphatic audacity he sang the practicability of his plan. 'Plastic tabs.' 'Plastics for the palace of the Mandarin.' 'Plaid plastics for Macbeth.' The placid inhabitants of Clacton stood abashed before the extravagant attitude of the Professor towards his plan. The graphic artists were apathetic to a man.

Exercise for ĕ
The vowel in 'said,' 'spread' [e]. Extreme pronunciations are either too 'open,' in which case the vowel resembles ă, or too 'close,' in which case it resembles AY. Do not spread the lips.

When the eccentric Gregory Kneller chose for his farewell performance *The Well of Death*, the tenth melodrama penned by Redvers Redvers, one of the theatre's greatest men of letters, his friends reprehended him. However, Kneller kept to his plans, and went so far as to spring a surprise in the letter scene, when he took the letter from a shelf up left. For, whereas he should have read it to himself, he let it fall, stepped dead centre, and spoke extempore, as if from memory, and addressed himself to the twelfth spectator in the second row of the dress circle. Interviewed next morning by a friendly member of the press who remarked on the resemblance this bore to another letter scene, he said he never read any plays but his own, and that Redvers Redvers concealed the identity of Gregory Kneller, a secret he had kept from the press throughout his seventy years on the West End stage.

Exercise for *AY*

The vowel in 'played,' 'they,' 'weigh' [eɪ] . Like *OH*, the sound *AY* is included in the list of simple vowels on the Resonator Scale, although it is strictly a diphthong. The sound begins, approximately, with the ĕ, as in bed, and the tongue rises towards ĭ, as in ship for the second element. In Scotland and many parts of the north this vowel is not diphthongized. The most frequent variations are in the starting point for this sound; sometimes starting with ă or even a sound near to *AH* as in certain varieties of Cockney. Do not spread the lips.

The way Miss Grace Sage defends the ancient stage is of the greatest interest to playgoers. She maintains the present day has little to take the place of the motive of fate. She hails the Greek way and would not fail to alienate actors who would not undertake to mask their faces and sustain a stately declamation throughout the pages of a play. In this way the stage could be saved, claims Miss Sage, by raising it to a more elevated plane. Grace Sage may be seen any day, vacantly making her way through Long Acre, swathed in a chaste cape of ancient grey marocaine, or parading with an air of disdain in the foyers of St. Martin's Lane.

Exercise for ĭ

The vowel in 'guild,' 'ship,' 'pity [ɪ]. When in final positions this vowel is often pronounced with too low a tongue position, the final vowel becoming almost an ĕ. The reverse is also frequently heard when the final ĭ becomes *EE*; 'city' in this case becomes 'citee.' The hall-mark of the crooner's diction! Extreme dialectal pronunciation gives a diphthong of the *er* + *i* [əɪ] type. Many words have an alternate pronunciation with the neutral *er* as in the third syllable of infinity. It is better to avoid this for the sake of clarity. Words like 'private,' 'locket,' 'horrible,' are better with ĭ than *er*. Final *ed* is always better with ĭ, i.e. 'actid' and not 'actered.' Do not spread the lips.

The prima donna's singing was admitted by a select audience to be all that could be wished, in that it was well-nigh perfect. Her diction was distinct, and admirably suited to the immense size of the gilded auditorium, which was beautifully lit. The electricians outdid themselves with the brilliant and elaborate lighting they had provided for the set. Six spots were riveted on the prima donna, ready to pick out the delicacy of her every movement, even to the flicker of an eyelid. Unfortunately, she was a believer in the beauty of extreme repose, and her acting tactics consisted of remaining ecstatically static, except when she tripped, when taking the fifth curtain. This admittedly was hardly fitting, but was forgiven, and indeed scarcely noticed, owing to the generosity and inimitable grace with which she acknowledged the plaudits of the distinguished gathering.

Witty Kitty McQuittey was a natty secretary to Sir Willy Gatty, the wholesale apothecary. She spoke excellently at the committee meetings of the fifty city companies in which Willy was financially interested. She principally excelled in very ably terminating the stodgy insipidity of Willy's addresses, and instinctively knew when to do this. She was singularly successful in skilfully countering the rivalry and duplicity of his enemies by cryptically and often elliptically rigging the market. This drove them scatty. In her spare time she was happy to assist Lady Gatty in her many charities. Truly the perfect secretary.

Exercise for *EE*
The vowel in 'weed,' 'police,' 'received' [iː]. This vowel is diphthongized by many people, the tongue starting from *ĭ* and sliding up to *EE*, which gives the *ĭ + EE* [ɪi] type. In marked dialectal pronunciations the tongue starts as low as *ER* which gives the pronunciation *sER + EE* [səɪ] for see. If the movement is very slight, it is allowable, but it is best to practise this vowel with no tongue movement whatsoever. Great care should be taken not to draw back the lips, and great care is necessary when *L* follows.

In Act III we see the deeds of the three chief leads revealed. Their chief aim has been to please Queen Louise. The scene depicts her enfeebled and weak, but with regal mien, seated on her throne on the quay at Deal, receiving them kneeling in profile, speechless at her feet. For their Queen, they have been pleased to cross the seas with her fleet to achieve her dream of seizing a new kingdom in the East. Beneath a sky of ultramarine, across which seagulls weave and screech, all three speak discreetly in tones steeped with feeling. The scene, to be believed, must be seen.

When *OO* is preceded by *Y*, the tongue is often brought too far forward, owing to the influence of the Y, giving rise to a dialectal pronunciation. There are many degrees of this. To correct an extreme pronunciation, the vowels *EE* and *OO* should be alternated with rapidity whilst concentrating on the two vowel positions. If the *YOO* sound is present to the mind in doing this, the incorrect movements will probably be made.

> Few new ballets are due at the New in June, but *European Unicorn* will be substituted for the amusing *Cuban Fugue*. The particularly tuneful music for tubas and lutes, somewhat in the style of Debussy, is suitably euphonious. Hugaroff uses his thews superbly as the semi-nude youth, and Eustanova luxuriates in the caprioles of the unicorn. The cubist decor is in beautifully subdued hues of fuchsia and petunia. Pursued by the infuriated unicorn, the unfortunate youth with acute ingenuity takes refuge behind a huge tulip-tree, which receives the unicorn's cornuted protuberance, in full view of innumerable supine and superfluous supernumeraries.

Exercise for *U*
The 'neutral' sound. The unstressed vowel in 'alone,' 'other,' 'sofa' [ə]. This sound, which is one of the most frequently used in any piece of English, occurs only in unstressed positions. It is a short sound and commonly used in weak forms of many words such as and [ənd] for [fə] but [bət]. When the neutral sound occurs finally in such words as other, rather, there may be a tendency to make a sound too near *AH*: this should be avoided.

Ample practice for this sound will be found in almost any piece of English prose where the reader speaks in an easy colloquial style.

COMPOUND VOWELS
These differ from the simple vowels in that they are gliding sounds, whereas the simple vowels demand a fixed and stable position throughout their utterance. In a compound vowel, the articulating organs start in the position of one vowel and immediately leave it and proceed in the direction of a second vowel. They are exceedingly difficult to describe on paper, especially as the majority of them do not start from exactly the same position as any of the simple vowels. Thus the vowel in 'high' does not start in the normal

AH position, nor does it start from the *ŭ* position, but from somewhere in between the two. This position has been indicated for these vowels as far as is humanly possible, but the ear is ultimately the only true guide. All the compound vowels in English are stressed on their first elements; an exception to this would have to be made in the case of the vowel group '*you*,' but the view taken in this book is that this sound is the vowel *OO* preceded by the consonant *Y*. All the compound vowels are monosyllabic in character, and if sung, the first element should be prolonged.

DIPHTHONGS AND TRIPHTHONGS
Compound vowels are usually divided into diphthongs and so-called triphthongs. As their name indicates, they are distinguished by the number of positions of the resonator involved. *I* and *OW*, when followed by the neutral form of *ER*, are usually considered as triphthongs. When *AY*, *OH*, and *OY* are followed by this vowel they are disyllabic and cannot, therefore, be so classed.

Exercise for *I*
The diphthong in 'sky,' 'high,' 'buy' [aɪ]. The tongue starts from a position roughly midway between *AH* and *ŭ* and moves towards *i*. It is not necessary fully to reach the *ĭ* position. Pronunciations range between the affected 'refaned' *ă* + *ĭ* [æɪ] type and the Cockney 'broad' *I* which starts on *AH*, or even from *ŏ*, resulting in a diphthong of the type *AH* + *ĭ* [aɪ]. This vowel is particularly liable to nasalization. It is often flattened when followed by L. In Yorkshire and Lancashire *I* starts approximately from *ŭ*, which is lengthened.

The Island in the Highlands is to be revived on Friday the ninth of July. Readers will like to be reminded of the delightfully surprising climax of this old-time melodrama. The final scene depicts the irate squire in a dim light, in the aisle of the ruined Byzantine chapel, on the Isle of Skye, where he holds captive Myra's child Simon, whose death he desires. He is about to fire a revolver between Simon's eyes when Myra enters with a wild cry, 'My child, My child.' With diabolical smile, the Squire fixes Myra with his fiery eyes. The skies are then rent with the sound of bagpipes. With a sigh of surprise he almost drops the child, which is caught in the nick of time by the McKay of McKay, who strikes the squire with an iron pike. He dies. Myra, Simon, and McKay

cry with delight, while the pipers play 'I'll meet you in Skye.'
Lyceum twice nightly at five and nine.

Exercise for *OW*

The diphthong in cloud,' 'now,' 'bough' [au] The starting place for
this vowel is somewhat in advance of *AH*. Pronounced with an *AH*,
it sounds exaggerated and affected. The position then changes to
that of *ōō*. A great many varieties are to be heard, ranging through *ĕ*,
AH, *ŏ*, and even *ER* as starting places [eu, ɑu, ɒu, əu]. Frequently
the lip rounding for the second element is omitted. In extremes of
London dialect, the second element is omitted altogether and the
tongue position for the first is advanced, in which case 'about'
becomes abaat [əbaːt].

'The Roundheads Carouse' is the resounding title chosen by
Professor MacLeod for this year's town pageant, which will be
mounted in the grounds of the Dower House, by kind permission
of Lady Brown. The crowning episode shows the Countess
Howard at sundown, against a set piece of mounting towers.
Seated on a mound, under the branching bough of an oak, she is
flanked by couchant boarhounds. Down right, the scowling
roundheads stand on a bed of downtrodden flowers. Down left,
the cowled monks lend their powerful aid. The Countess coun-
ters the mounting fury of the Roundheads by her cloudless brow,
as they command her to surrender the crown. In a profound and
lowering silence she propounds 'Not for a thousand pounds.' The
ensuing silence is broken only by the hooting of downy owls from
a flowery bower and the cowbells of the browsing cows.

TRIPHTHONGS

'Our' and 'ire' are frequently 'flattened.' That is, the second position
of these triphthongs is not made sufficiently prominent in which
case 'our' becomes almost *AH* + *er* [ɑə] and 'ire' becomes *AH* + *er*
[ɑə]. Such speakers would refer to the 'tar on their tars' and to both
'empire' and 'empower' as 'empah!' In correcting this 'flattened'
formation considerable care must be taken to preserve the monosyllabic nature of these sounds. They must not sound like 'i-yer'
[ajə] and 'ow-wer' [awə], which would be the case were the second
element to become too prominent.

par	power	pyre
bar	bower	byre
tar	tower	tire
car	cower	crier
far	flower	fire
Shah	shower	shire
jar	Giaour	gyre
lance	allowance	alliance
marble	allowable	liable

Exercise for *OY*

The diphthong in 'ahoy,' 'coil,' 'box' [ɔɪ]. The starting place is a little difficult to define. It is roughly half-way between ŏ and *AW*. Care must be taken to avoid rounding the lips more than for *AW*, and never to have less lip rounding than for ŏ.

Moya Malloy, after enjoying unalloyed popularity, has retired from the boisterous noise and the toil and moil of London to loiter the rest of her days in Croyde. Here, without annoy, she enjoys royal seclusion by boycotting the *hoi polloi*, and indulges her poignant liking for playing quoits in corduroys in a coign of her garden. One of her little foibles is to don a flamboyant coif and drive a carefully oiled and noiseless troika with adroit poise. 'Hoity-toity' call the hoydens and hobbledehoys of Croyde.

Exercise for *EAR*

The diphthong in 'peer,' 'pier,' 'rear' [ɪə]. The starting place is exercise ĭ, page 108. The tongue then proceeds to a vowel slightly lower in position than *ER*. The tongue must never be allowed to reach the ŭ position, which would result in the affected pronunciation usually represented by 'heah!' An intrusive *Y* must not be heard, i.e. 'pee yer.' [pɪjə]. In 'standard' pronunciation, the *R* is silent. In Scottish the *EE* sound is heard followed by a rolled *R*. Elsewhere, a frictionless *R* may be heard, or the consonant may be pronounced simultaneously with the vowel. This treatment of the *R* applies to the remaining diphthongs and will not be referred to again.

Brereton Lear reappears every year never weary of portraying the Indian Vizier. He is revered for the mysterious, superior atmosphere he creates as, with queer, bleary leers, he steers the inexperienced Vera, and the tearful Victoria, quaking with fear, nearer and nearer to the sheer edge of the cheerless weir, where stands the sneering, imperial Emir.

Exercise for *AIR*

The diphthong in 'fair,' 'their,' 'pear' [ɛə]. The starting place is approximately ĕ (see p. 107). Although a slightly lower position is admissible, it must never be so low as ă. Avoid 'faiah' and the intrusive *Y* – 'fai yer'. In some parts of the north and the midlands a 'flattened' variety between ĕ and *ER* is heard. In Scottish, a simple vowel is heard, which is slightly more 'closed' than ĕ.

Fair and Square is everywhere declared to be unbearably daring. Mary Baird, the dairymaid, disgraced by the Laird's heir, wears her cares with rare bearing. We see her descend the stairs with a careless air with her pair of fair-haired bairns. Bare-headed, barefoot and in despair, she stares at a chair, ere she utters a prayer, whilst carelessly tearing her bairns' fair hair.

Exercise for *OOR*

The diphthong in 'tour,' 'sure,' 'poor' [uə]. The first position is that of ŏŏ. The tongue then moves to the neutral *ER*, slightly lower in position as in the case of 'here' and 'there.' No intrusive *W* should be heard – 'poo-wer' [puwə]. Care should be taken that the tongue does not start from the *AW* position. As with 'here' and 'there,' the Scottish use a simple vowel and roll the *R*, while in the north and south-west, the diphthong is followed by an untrilled *R*. The *R* is silent in 'standard' pronunciation. This sound is more appropriately retained in classical roles since it is rapidly losing currency in everyday conversational speech.

The search for the Ruritanian crown jewels ends on the Cornish moors near Truro. Poor Muriel is immured with the neurotic McClure in a sort of Moorish Kursaal hung with lurid murals. Alluring in pure white tulle, she watches him casually secreting the jewels in a bureau. Steeling herself to abjure his boorish advances, she is reassured by the horn of the dour, but romantic, Stewart's six-cylinder tourer. He creates a furore in bursting open the door, and endures a gruelling, but effectual, duel with the infuriated McClure.

There remains the vowel sound in words like 'sore' and 'wore.' In many people's pronunciation there is no difference made between words ending in *ore* and those ending in *aw*, so that 'saw' and 'sore' are identical. On the other hand, in some parts of the country a distinction is made. Whether one is to distinguish between 'paw' and 'pore' is largely a matter of taste and preference, and it is not simple to give a ruling. Those who already distinguish between them must beware of making the 'ore' words markedly diphthongal, for this is a distinguishing feature of the dialectal pronunciation of these sounds. 'Ore' demands more a slackening of the lip shaping than a definite move in the direction of *ER*. Great care, however, must be taken over 'oor' and 'our' words, as these are more frequently than not reduced to the level of the 'aw' words by all classes of speakers. All three sounds may be practised in the following lists –

paw	pore	poor	law	lore	Lourdes
awe	bore	boor	for	four	petits fours
taw	tore	tour	maw	more	moor
daw	door	dour	raw	roar	rural
caw	core	gourd	shaw	shore	sure
war	wore	wooer	yawl	yore	your

Many a Claudius has failed to distinguish between a state of mind and the time of day –

> 'Tis sweet and commendable in your nature, Hamlet,
> To give these mourning duties to your father:
> > (*Hamlet*, I. ii.)

and Portia has been heard to lapse from grace by offending the ears of her new found love –

> One half of me is yours, the other half yours –
> Mine own, I would say; but if mine, then yours,
> And so all yours!
> > (*The Merchant of Venice*, III. ii.)

INTRUSIVE GLIDES

As we have seen, a compound vowel is the result of the gliding movement of the tongue and lips passing from one position to another. In connected speech, the articulation organs must of necessity pass through all the intermediate positions between one sound and another. It is a fault in delivery when these glides become audible. They are most likely to be heard when one word ends and the next begins with a vowel, especially when OO and *oo* are followed by a vowel, in which case an intrusive *W* is heard. When *EE, i, AY* are followed by a vowel, the intrusive glide is *Y* –

so easy	*not*	so wheezy	to all	*not*	to wall
so eerie	*not*	so weary	how awed	*not*	how warred
to wear	*not*	to air	see all	*not*	sea yawl
the ear	*not*	the year	the oak	*not*	the yoke

The difficulties of the first list must not be surmounted by having recourse to the glottal explosive, which would give 'so ?easy,' 'see ?over,' etc., but by perfect timing of the stress. The stress must be given at the moment of shaping for the second vowel of each pair, and the tongue and lips must not exceed the limit of the movements for the vowel of the preceding word. 'The ox, the ass, and the owl,' and not 'the yox, the yass, and the yowl.'

Imperfect timing of stress also causes the detachment of a consonant from the preceding syllable, so that it gives the impression of belonging to a following word, e.g. 'thi sis the firs tan donly.' Take care to avoid these intrusive vowel glides in the following example –

Sir Hugo Ely, the operatic impressario, revealed his plans to me the other day, as he showed me over the new opera house which will be opened in early October, when the opera will be *Aida*. Sir Hugo always maintains there is no object in being too ornate or too eager to assault the ear throughout the three acts of this or any other opera. He plans to make the whole thing easy on the eye as well as on the ear. 'How interesting it has been to meet you,' said Hugo, as he saw me out. 'May I say how eager we all are to invite you and your colleagues to the opening night?'

SIMPLIFICATIONS

Speech sounds influence each other to a marked degree when they meet in connected speech. The pronunciation of a language is a record of the influences sounds have had on each other. The tendency has been, and still is, to simplify the speech movements when these are at all complex. Speakers fail to achieve the necessary delicacy of the minute movements of the speech organs, and a fresh, simplified pronunciation is gradually evolved. A great many of these simplifications are admissible through custom, but those which have not passed into current usage are inadmissible. There are many cases where pronunciation is hovering between what was said, and what is said. Recommendations in these cases are difficult.

The most obvious simplification occurs in the omission of sounds when two or more consonants are in juxtaposition. Thus the italicized sounds are regularly omitted from 'gran*d*mother, han*d*-kerchief, Chris*t*mas, wais*t*coat, han*d*some,' and to replace them would be pedanticism in its worst form. Striking examples of this form of simplification are to be found in colloquial usage, e.g. 'bed n breakfast,' 'bread n butter,' 'cup n saucer,' or even 'bread m butter.' Such simplifications must be heard from the actor only when they are indicative of the speech habits of the characters of the play.

SPELLING PRONUNCIATION

The opposite tendency is heard in the attempt to make the pronunciation of words match their spelling, and so to replace sounds whose omission custom has sanctioned. This often has a most ludicrous effect, and gives rise to the expression 'spelling pronunciation.' It was customary in the past to omit the *H* in, for example, the words 'herb,' 'humour,' and 'hospital.' The spelling of the words has influenced pronunciation, and the *H* has come into its own again, the process having been arrested in the case of 'heir,' 'honest,' 'hour' and their derivatives. Custom, therefore, decides in the case of this consonant. But the influence of spelling is seen at its most absurd in the case of vowels in unstressed syllables, when their stressed values are given to the italicized vowels in such words as 'gard*e*n,' 'sail*o*r,' 'pavem*e*nt,' making them rhyme with 'den,' 'law,' and 'meant.'

Pronunciation changes, and is never set and fixed from age to age. Current pronunciations are the result of evolutionary processes, whereby difficulties in articulation have been solved by simplification, in the remote or more immediate past. Spelling, on the other hand, does not change to such a marked degree and is now to all intents and purposes fixed. Pronunciation and spelling, therefore, often bear no resemblance to each other. The individual is not free to make the one accord with the other. Custom is the authority in such matters, and where specific pronunciations have become established it is not only ridiculous but pedantic to swim against the current.

The tendency to simplify the movements made by the tongue is ever present. When these are at all difficult, and omission of a sound is not possible, a compromise in movement is made. Some of these compromises have come to be accepted, but the majority of those usually heard are inadmissible. Thus 'nature,' 'feature,' 'picture,' and others of the same group were all at one time pronounced 'natioor,' 'featioor,' 'pictioor.' The simplifications to 'nacher,' 'pickcher,' and 'feacher' have become accepted. To say 'natioor' would nowadays merely call undue attention to the manner in which the word was being pronounced, and would lead to the speaker being branded as affected. But what of these words in the following contexts –

> 'Tis beauty truly blent, whose red and white
> Nature's own sweet and cunning hand laid on:
> > (*Twelfth Night*, I. v.)

> . . . for anything so overdone is from the purpose of playing, whose end, both at the first and now, was and is, to hold, as 'twere, the mirror up to nature; to show virtue her own feature, scorn her own image, and the very age and body of the time his form and pressure.
> > (*Hamlet*, III. ii.)

> Look here, upon this picture, and on this.
> > (*Hamlet*, III. iv.)

In these cases it is necessary to compromise by avoiding the pedanticism of 'natioor,' as well as the colloquialism of 'nacher,' and this is the solution adopted by the judicious.

'Nation' and words ending in 'tion' were at one time spoken as 'nasiown.' It is often necessary to preserve a modified form of this pronunciation in verse, when the full syllabic utterance of the line makes 'nashun' impossible –

> Raining the tears of lamentation.
> > (*Love's Labour's Lost*, V. ii.)

> Thou hast seal'd up my expectation.
> > (*Henry IV*, II. IV. iv.)

All these words have a similar feature in that the short cuts have been made in unstressed syllables. In stressed syllables, the careless speaker will take full advantage of the situation and lapse into the laziness of –

chube	*for*	tube	jupe	*for*	dupe
machewer	*for*	mature	jew	*for*	due
chune	*for*	tune	juring	*for*	during
chumult	*for*	tumult			

although the latter would probably be indicated more correctly by 'jawring!' In colloquial speech, pairs of words suffer in the same way. 'I'll meet you' becomes 'I'll meechoo.' 'Would you mind?' becomes 'Woojoo mind?' 'Immediate,' 'hideous,' 'tedious,' 'perfidious,' are all subject to the same ill-treatment. Full value should be given to all their sounds, but the simplification is admissible in 'righteous.'

'Celestial,' 'bestial,' and all other 'tial' words must not degenerate into the 'beschl' pronunciation of 'celeschl.' 'Presume' and 'resume' as 'prezoom' and 'rezoom,' and 'sued' and 'suit' as 'sood' and 'soot' are illustrations of the careless omission of *y* which should always be included in these words.

> . . . for let the world take note,
> You are the most immediate to our throne
>
> (*Hamlet*, I. ii.)

> With that, methought, a legion of foul fiends
> Environed me about, and howled in mine ears
> Such hideous cries, that with the very noise
> I trembling waked . . .
>
> (*Richard III*, I. iv.)

> 'A tedious brief scene of young Pyramus
> And his love Thisbe; very tragical mirth.'
> Merry and tragical! tedious and brief!
>
> (*A Midsummer Night's Dream*, V. i.)

> So lust, though to a radiant angel linkt,
> Will sate itself in a celestial bed,
> And prey on garbage.
>
> (*Hamlet*, I. v.)

Now whether it be
Bestial oblivion, or some craven scruple
Of thinking too precisely on th' event, . . .

> (*Hamlet*, IV. iv.)

Do not presume too much upon my love;
I may do that I shall be sorry for.

> (*Julius Caesar*, IV. iii.)

Of a strange nature is the suit you follow.

> (*Merchant of Venice*, IV. i.)

The very stones prate of my whereabout,
And take the present horror from the time,
Which now suits with it.

> (*Macbeth*, II. i.)

We are left with 'issue' and 'tissue.' The pronunciations 'ishoo' and 'tishoo' are true examples of simplifications by short cuts and may, perhaps, be justifiably heard in Noel Coward, but what of –

' 'Tis not the balm, the sceptre and the ball,
The sword, the mace, the crown imperial,
The intertissued robe of gold and pearl . . .'

> (*Henry V*, IV. i.)

and

She did lie
In her pavilion; – cloth-of-gold of tissue

> (*Antony and Cleopatra*, II. ii)

The following example gives ample opportunity for either avoiding or making these simplifications –

Julia was actually due to be married to the Duke of Turin on the first Tuesday in June. It was naturally assumed by the multitude that she would eventually appear to receive their tumultuous greetings, suitably attired, and presumably wearing her superb jewels. But when the great day duly arrived, Julia's mature duenna could not produce the jewels. A duologue ensued, during which

Julia deduced they had been stolen, but the duenna was dubious, assumed the reverse, and immediately instituted a search. Julia felt suicidal, for at that moment the Duke, pursuant to his promise, had dutifully started a ducal serenade with a superfluous but celestially tuneful Tudor tune played on lutes and flutes, thus studiously pressing his suit to the last. Eventually a substitute was found, owing to the duenna's aptitude for superhuman and enduring efforts, actuated by a combination of duty and gratitude.

ARTICULATION AND PACE

There is one further aspect of articulation to be considered. It must obviously be able to stand up to the pace which is demanded, not only by general considerations but also by the technical use of pace in relation to emotional or situational contexts. Clarity is relatively easy to attain when speech is taken at a general mean pace, but it cannot be assumed that articulation will stand the strain of the reverse condition, unless the actor has developed the power of speaking clearly at a greater pace than is ever likely to be required.

EXERCISES FOR PACE

The passages given below are to be regarded as articulatory fences which are to be taken at an extremely rapid pace. All movements which are difficult by reason of the juxtaposition of certain consonants, or by a rapid succession of unstressed syllables, should be lifted out of their context and practised separately until the necessary agility is acquired. Every syllable is to be formed and given its due value.

Each passage must be pointed in such a way as to convey its full implications, but in doing this the pace must not be sacrificed. They should not be treated as exercises on mere rapidity but on rapidity and dramatic intention in equal proportions. Phrasing will obviously be of great importance, and the places where breath is to be taken should be worked out in the course of practice.

Each passage is first of all to be whispered, with the intention of conveying the meaning by means of the clarity of the articulatory movement alone. The minimum amount of voice possible is then to be introduced, still concentrating on the light, forward articulation of the whole. Gradually increase the volume and the pace, until each can be spoken with extreme rapidity without loss of clarity.

Exercise 1

Rats!
They fought the dogs, and killed the cats,
And bit the babies in the cradles,
And ate the cheeses out of the vats,
And licked the soup from the cooks' own ladles,
Split open the kegs of salted sprats,
Made nests inside men's Sunday hats,
And even spoiled the women's chats,
　　　By drowning their speaking
　　　With shrieking and squeaking
In fifty different sharps and flats.
　　　　　　　(*The Pied Piper of Hamelin* – Robert Browning.)

Exercise 2

Great rats, small rats, lean rats, brawny rats,
Brown rats, black rats, grey rats, tawny rats,
Grave old plodders, gay young friskers,
　　　Fathers, mothers, uncles, cousins,

Cocking tails and pricking whiskers,
　　　Families by tens and dozens,
Brothers, sisters, husbands, wives –
Followed the piper for their lives.

　　　　　　　　　　　　　　　(*Ibid.*)

Exercise 3

The fox was strong, he was full of running,
He could run for an hour and then be cunning,
But the cry behind him made him chill,
They were nearer now and they meant to kill.
They meant to run him until his blood
Clogged on his heart as his brush with mud,
Till his back bent up and hid tongue hung flagging,
And his belly and brush were filthed from dragging.
Till he crouched stone-still, dead-beat and dirty,
With nothing but teeth against the thirty.
And all the way to that blinding end
He would meet with men and have none his friend:
Men to holloa and men to run him,

With stones to stagger and yells to stun him;
Men to head him, with whips to beat him,
Teeth to mangle and mouths to eat him
And all the way, that wild high crying.
To cold his blood with the thought of dying,
The horn and the cheer, and the drum-like thunder
Of the horsehooves stamping the meadow under.

(*Reynard the Fox* – John Masefield.)

Exercise 4

Valentine. Why, how know you that I am in love?

Speed. Marry, by these special marks: first, you have learn'd, like Sir Proteus, to wreathe your arms, like a malcontent; to relish a love-song like a robin-redbreast; to walk alone, like one that had the pestilence; to sigh, like a school-boy that has lost his A B C; to weep, like a young wench that had buried her grandam; to fast, like one that takes diet; to watch, like one that fears robbing; to speak puling, like a beggar at Hallowmas. You were wont, when you laugh'd, to crow like a cock; when you walk'd, to walk like one of the lions; when you fasted, it was presently after dinner; when you look'd sadly, it was for want of money: and now you are metamorphosed with a mistress, that, when I look on you, I can hardly think you are my master.

(*The 'Two Gentleman of Verona'*, II. i.)

Exercise 5

Biondello. Why, Petruchio is coming, in a new hat and an old jerkin; a pair of old breeches, thrice turn'd; a pair of boots that have been candle-cases, one buckled, another laced; an old rusty sword ta'en out of the town armoury, with a broken hilt, and chapeless; with two broken points: his horse hipt with an old mothy saddle, and stirrups of no kindred; besides, possest with the glanders, and like to mose in the chine; troubled with the lampass infected with the fashions, full of windgalls, sped with spavins, ray'd with the yellows, past cure of the fives, stark spoil'd with the staggers, begnawn with the bots; sway'd in the back, and shoulder-shotten; near-legg'd before, and with a half-cheek bit, and a headstall of sheep's leather, which, being restrain'd to keep him from stumbling, hath been often burst, and new-repair'd with knots; one girth six times pieced, and a woman' crupper of velure, which hath two letters for her name fairly set down in studs, and here and there pieced with packthread.

(The Taming of the Shrew, III. ii.)

A dictionary is advisable!

Exercise 6

Puff. I daresay now you conceive half the very civil paragraphs and advertisements you see, to be written by the parties concerned, or their friends? No such thing. Nine times out of ten, manufactured by me in the way of business.

Sneer. Indeed!

Puff. Even the auctioneers now – the auctioneers, I say, though the rogues have lately got some credit for their language – not an article of the merit theirs! – take them out of their pulpits, and they are as dull as catalogues! – No, sir; 'twas I first enriched their style – 'twas I first taught them to crowd their advertisements with panegyrical superlatives each epithet rising above the other like the bidders in their own auctionrooms! From me they learned to inlay their phraseology with variegated chips of exotic metaphor: by me too their inventive faculties were called forth. Yes, sir, by me they were instructed to clothe ideal walls with gratuitous fruit – to insinuate obsequious rivulets into visionary groves – to teach courteous shrubs to nod their approbation of the grateful soil! or on emergencies to raise upstart oaks, where there never had been an acorn; to create a delightful vicinage without the assistance of a neighbour; or to fix the temple of Hygeia in the fens of Lincolnshire!

(The Critic, I. ii.)

Exercise 7

Lovemore. If they do bridle and hold a little, the struggle they undergo is the most ridiculous sight in nature. I have seen a huge oath quivering on the pale lip of a reigning toast for half an hour together, and an uplifted eye accusing the gods for the lots of an odd trick. And then, at last, the whole room in a Babel of sounds. 'My lord, you flung away the game – Sir George, why did not you rough the spade? Captain Hazard, why did not you lead through the honours – Ma'am, it was not the play – Pardon me, sir – but ma'am, – but sir – I would not play with you or straws; don't you know what Hoyle says? – If A and B are partners against C and D, and the game nine all, A and B have won three tricks, and C and D four tricks; C leads his suit, D puts up the king then returns the suit, A passes, C puts up the queen, and B trumps it; and so A and B, and C and D are bandied about, they attack, they defend, and all is jargon and confusion, wrangling, noise and nonsense; and high life, and polite conversation.

(*The Way to Keep Him* – Arthur Murphy.)

Exercise 8

Tolkatchov. I have five lists in my pocket, and my handkerchief is nothing but knots. And so, my dear fellow, in the time between the office and the train, one's tearing about the town like a dog with its tongue out – tearing about and cursing one's life. From the draper's to the chemist's, from the chemist's to the dress-maker's, from the dressmaker's to the pork butcher's, and then back to the chemist's again. In one place you trip up, in another you lose your money, in the third you forget to pay and they run after you and make a row, in the fourth you tread on a lady's skirt ... pfoo! Such a form of exercise sends one dotty and makes one such a wreck that every bone aches all night afterwards, and one dreams of crocodiles. Well, your tasks have been performed and everything has been bought – now kindly tell me how is one to pack all this truck? How, for instance, are you going to pack a heavy copper pan and a mortar with a globe for the lamp, or carbolic with tea? How are you going to combine bottles of beer and a bicycle?

(*An Unwilling Martyr* – Anton Tchekhov.)

SYLLABIFICATION

The omission of syllables is not a matter on which an inflexible ruling can be given. Whether omission of syllables is permissible or not, depends, as do so many of the other aspects already discussed, upon the mode of speech which the actor is required to reproduce. In the conversational delivery of everyday life unstressed syllables are omitted with great frequency, chiefly in polysyllabic words, and no great harm is done. In a play in which dialogue reproduces the effect of this conversational mode it would be unwise to go the whole hog by giving every unstressed syllable equal value.

In Shakespeare, on the other hand, in fact in all plays written in verse, their omission will often completely destroy the rhythm which orders their progression. The most notable examples of this are to be found in the necessity to give full value to the 'ed' of the past participle.

> Proceeding from the heat oppressed brain.
>> (*Macbeth*, II, i.)

> Thy brother by decree is banished.
>> (*Julius Caesar*, III. i.)

This line immediately recalls what is demanded of a Romeo and Juliet in Act III, Scenes 2 and 3 where Romeo has an indication of both pronunciations.

> Hence banished is banish't from the world.

The elision of syllables, however, is most likely to occur in words ending in 'ery' and 'ary,' and in those which contain an unstressed 'er' medially.

> Might fire the blood of ordinary men.
>> (*Caesar*, III. i.)

> My credit now stands on such slippery ground,
> That one of two bad ways you must conceit me,
> Either a coward, or a flatterer.
>> (*Ibid.*)

> With all kind love, good thoughts, and reverence.   (*Ibid.*)

But such omissions are the result not merely of laziness in syllabification, but of an ear which is deaf to the rhythmic implications of the verse.

EXERCISES FOR SYLLABIFICATION

Of the passages that follow, one serves as a model of what is required in the way of normal syllabification, and the others of the amusing effect which may be obtained by syllabic utterance. All of these are excellent exercises and demand much agility when taken at a smart pace.

Exercise 1

At this fusty stuff
The large Achilles, on his presst bed lolling,
From his deep chest laughs out a loud applause;
Cries, 'Excellent! 'tis Agamemnon just.
Now play me Nestor; hem, and stroke thy beard,
As he being drest to some oration.'
That's done – as near as the extremest ends
Of parallels; as like as Vulcan and his wife:
Yet god Achilles still cries, 'Excellent!
'Tis Nestor right. Now play him me, Patroclus,
Arming to answer in a night-alarm.'
And then, forsooth, the faint defects of age
Must be the scene of mirth; to cough and spit,
And, with a palsy fumbling on his gorget,
Shake in and out the rivet – and at this sport
Sir Valour dies; cries, 'O, enough, Patroclus;
Or give me ribs of steel! I shall split all
In pleasure of my spleen.' And in this fashion,
All our abilities, gifts, natures, shapes,
Severals and generals of grace exact,
Achievements, plots, orders, preventions,
Excitements to the field, or speech for truce,
Success or loss, what is or is not, serves
As stuff for these two to make paradoxes.
                                    (*Troilus and Cressida*, I., iii.)

Exercise 2

I am the very model of a modern Major-General
I've information vegetable, animal and mineral,
I know the Kings of England, and I quote the fights historical,
From Marathon to Waterloo, in order categorical;
I'm very well acquainted too with matters mathematical,
I understand equations, both the simple and quadratical,
About binomial theorem I'm teeming with a lot o' news –
With many cheerful facts about the square of the hypotenuse.
I'm very good at integral and differential calculus,
I know the scientific names of beings animalculous;
In short, in matters vegetable, animal and mineral,
I am the very model of a modern Major-General.
                                    (W. S. Gilbert.)

Exercise 3

My eyes are fully open to my awful situation
I shall go at once to Roderic and make him an oration.
I shall tell him I've recovered my forgotten moral senses,
And I don't care twopence halfpenny for any consequences.
Now I do not want to perish by the sword or by the dagger,
But a martyr may indulge a little pardonable swagger,
And a word or two of compliment my vanity would flatter,
But I've got to die to-morrow, so it really doesn't matter.

If I had been so lucky as to have a steady brother
Who could talk to me, as we are talking, now, to one another,
Who could give me good advice when he discovered I was erring
(Which is just the very favour which on you I am conferring),
My story would have made a rather interesting idyll,
And I might have lived and died a very decent indiwiddle,
This particularly rapid, unintelligible patter
Isn't generally heard, and if it is, it doesn't matter.

                                                    (W. S. Gilbert.)

7 · CONCLUSION

During the course of this book, great emphasis has been laid upon voice and speech, since these two, which meet in utterance, form the very core of the actor's art. Yet, in the theatre, utterance should be so perfectly adapted to character and situation, and the conditions under which the performance takes place, that the audience, becoming absorbed in the action of the play, whether this be outward or inward, cease to notice the means, at any rate the vocal means, by which they are affected. It was remarked earlier, that utterance is a means to an end.

> The voice must be the servant of the actor's will and feeling, and anything in the voice which calls attention to itself, either because the actor appears to be voice conscious, or because the utterance is defective in some respect, will make a performance bad, shallow, or otherwise unconvincing. Technique and imagination must become one, and in the theatre both are dependent upon each other.

This unifying of technique and the expression of feeling can best be brought about by thinking of the whole of speech as being motivated by the intellect and emotions.

IMPORTANCE OF ARTICULATION
Attention has been directed to the relation between articulation and meaning, and the relation between tone and feeling. Thought and feeling must now be considered to be one with articulation. It is well-known that the technically accomplished can recite the alphabet, and at the same time convincingly portray, for example, the emotions of joy or grief. And yet such a performance makes no intellectual impact on the hearer. The emotion does not take precise shape, because the jumble of vowels and consonants that the recitation of the alphabet involves bears no relation to the combination of letters and sounds with which we are familiar in the words of our language. Neither has the alphabet any grammatical structure!

When Romeo first believes that Juliet is dead, he is so stricken with grief that he says –

Well, Juliet, I will lie with thee to-night.

The words have a tragic irony, but we are not yet sure of their full purport. It is not until we hear –

O mischief, thou art swift
To enter in the thoughts of desperate men!

that his emotion indicates his true purpose. Isolate the vowels in these words, and the lines mean nothing, and the emotion cannot be conveyed. Isolate the consonants, and there is a very different story to tell, and this can be represented to the eye –

- m-sch- -f, th- - -rt sw-ft
T- -nt-r -n th- th- -ghts -f d-sp-r-t- m-n.

The emotion resides in the tone, and the meaning in the articulation. Unite them, and the emotion is channelled by the words and brought into focus. It is the articulation which is responsible for this. That this is so, may be proved by whispering the lines on the breath with the intention of conveying the feeling. You will find that this can be done, for although the emotion cannot be communicated because the tone is absent, it can be experienced, always providing a distinct intention of what is to be conveyed is present to the mind. One attempts to achieve the impossible, i.e. to convey the feeling by means of the articulation. This way of regarding the matter, not only in theory, but also in practice, is an effective means of giving to words that freshness, spontaneity, and vitality which all stage utterance demands. The sensation should be that the thought and feeling come right forward on to the lips. This is really the mental counterpart of the technical aspect of forward diction. One not only speaks forward, but thinks forward! To speak forward will help in bringing the thought forward, and to think forward will help in bringing the utterance forward. Both processes are mutually dependent. Speak the lines aloud, and the tone which is set up will carry the articulation in which meaning resides and which gives definition to the emotion, to the farthest recesses of a theatre.

AUDIBILITY

To the farthest recesses of a theatre! If the conditions under which an actor performs are not to dwarf and smother their conception of a character, everything they do, including their utterance, must be larger than life. This problem has existed from the earliest times. The Greeks solved it by evolving a highly stylized form of utterance and movement, which must, in part, have been conditioned by the hampering effect of the tragic actor's costume. Even so, and allowing for the funnelling of the voice by the mask, the mere delivery of the actor's hexameters in vast open-air theatres must have demanded the most rigorous training in breath, note, tone, and word, and almost superhuman staying powers in performance. Now, the majority of naturalistic plays are often presented in theatres whose size is conditioned more by economic than by aesthetic considerations, so that even when a play is written, and its production designed, to convey an impression of truth to life, the fallacy of this claim is brought home when the actor is heard in all parts of the theatre: if it were true to life they would not be heard. This is a very real and an ever-present problem. That it must have existed over two thousand years ago we have seen, but for the English theatre the problem did not really exist until the playhouses assumed their present-day proportions, since it was not until the nineteenth century that size was considered to be an important feature of a theatre. In very large playhouses subtlety of effect becomes an impossibility. To overcome these conditions, the small, ill-defined everyday movements of real life must, for the stage, be designed and have breadth, in order that they may be seen effectively and acquire significance. Similarly, utterance must be magnified in all its aspects in order effectively to be heard.

PROJECTION

This aspect of utterance is included under the term projection. Projection of voice is necessary for one reason only, namely, that the actor's conception should 'Get Across.' It has been insisted that mere voice (in large theatres it is often a case of sheer voice) means nothing at all. The voice, then, must not be projected for its own sake, but solely in order to project the thought. This being so, the closer the relationship between the mental processes and utterance, the better. A marriage between the two must be brought about. For the voice is the principal, although not the only link between the stage and the auditorium, and just as the external action of a play must appear to spring directly from the inner, mental action of the characters, so must the thought of the actor appear to prompt and bring about utterance itself. Only then does utterance become convincing, and only then can it become moving. The technical means of approach to this ideal has been indicated. We must now pass to the technical aspect of projection. The first question that arises is that of audibility, since it is obvious that nothing can be conveyed by means of utterance unless this is distinctly audible. This problem of audibility is ever present to the actor, for, even when the utterance is above reproach, it must always be adapted to the acoustics of the theatre in which he or she is speaking. It is a case of tuning the instrument for performance. Even a Stradivarius needs to be tuned.

SUMMARY OF IMPORTANT FACTORS

Some indication has been given in these pages of the way in which each factor of utterance contributes towards audibility, but they must here be passed in review. The whole structure will fall to the ground if the breathing does not support the note, the tone, and the word. The first two cannot even exist without the breath, and the word can be made to carry only a very small distance by the use of the whispered voice. Rib-reserve is the answer to audibility as far as this depends upon breathing, for, by maintaining a reserve in the lungs, one always has breath upon which to fall back in the event of a particularly long phrase, and there is always sufficient to support each phrase-end in emphatic or unemphatic delivery. A tailing-off of breath pressure will inevitably give rise to inaudibility.

SUFFICIENT TONE

Clearly there must in general be a sufficiency of tone, principally for the purpose of carrying the articulation, but if audibility were dependent upon mere volume of tone, it would be impossible to get a scene over without recourse to shouting. Shouting should never be resorted to unless demanded by a specific situation, and, even then, there is a right and a wrong way to go about it. The advice 'shout from the stomach' is anatomically confusing, but contains a very large grain of truth, for the inexperienced will shout by means of tension and so will most efficiently box-up the tone they wish to produce. Always shout 'on the breath,' and by means of firm pressure at the base of the lungs.

DICTION

To project successfully, and yet not obviously, one must have 'forward' diction. The articulatory aspect of this has been reviewed. The tone must be aesthetically satisfying and gratify the ear, but must never be such that the character of the vowel is blurred. The essence of the sections in this book dealing with tone is that, when the tone is full, the positions for each vowel can be placed far forward in the mouth, which gives a bright forward ring to the character of the vowel, and this principle is illustrated and achieved by means of the resonator scale. If the placing of the tone is so far back as to appear muddy, it will always be a struggle to get the thought 'across.'

But each part of the voice depends upon the other, and even if the breathing is perfect and forward diction present, inaudibility will result unless precision of articulation exists. Audibility, then, is gained principally by governing the voice at its extremities; and the recipe for success in projection is to become conscious of one's vocal extremities and, once the tone is full, easy, and given a forward linguistic character, to keep it buoyant and responsive.

INFLECTION

But audibility depends also upon the technical management of inflection.

Discussion of this aspect of the note has been reserved for this chapter. It is well-known that in speaking the voice does not jump from note to note as it does in singing, but glides through a whole series of notes in making inflections. The separate notes of these inflections are indistinguishable. Discussion of inflection involves the voice only to a limited extent, as this element of utterance is referable more to the logical and emotional than to the vocal aspect of interpretation. The mere reproduction of an inflectional pattern will strike hollow if the thought and feeling which give rise to the pattern are not present.

Voice and mind are seen to be inter-dependent if the finest results are to be achieved. There must be not only a voice but a mind to direct it, and the highest effect will result only when both are balanced in equal proportion. The voice, however perfect, will never touch the heights unless it is directed by a sensitive perception of the meaning and emotion to be conveyed, and these will be cabin'd, cribb'd, and confined, if the voice has not a high degree of flexibility to give them release.

SPONTANEITY

It would be possible to reduce inflection to a series of rules, a method employed in the past by some who had more application than wisdom. Such a method is stultifying in the extreme, and would be the negation of one of the most vital qualities which should be possessed by every actor – spontaneity. When, therefore, the voice can be technically managed along the lines indicated, it acquires a disciplined freedom; disciplined in the sense that it is correctly managed and controlled, free in the sense that it is flexible, pliant, and responsive to the intention. When this is so, it is necessary that a part should be studied from the inside outwardly, and not in the reverse order.

On the other hand, there are speeches which are entirely intellectual in content, and these, if interest is not to flag, not only must be 'pointed' to convey the thread of the argument but must be kept alive by variety of pitch and inflection, and by all the attributes of delivery.

SUSTAINING THOUGHT AND TONE

In a major speech of any length the thought must be sustained. The voice plays a great part in doing this. Sustained tone having already been acquired, each section of a speech may be given its due value and related to the whole, so that the complete speech is received as a single complex thought, to which all the subsidiary thoughts contribute. If each phrase or each thought is given finality by means of inflection, the impression will be of a series of unconnected thoughts, instead of which, each thought should grow out of that which precedes it.

There are innumerable illustrations of this particular problem: Gloster in *Henry VI*, Part III, III. ii; Queen Margaret in *Henry VI*, Part III, V. iv, and from the rhetoric of these to the figures of the tragedies, through Romeo and Juliet to the Macbeths.

INFLECTION

In spite of the foregoing, certain technical aspects of inflection must be discussed, as audibility depends to a large extent upon the way some inflections are managed. English demands, broadly speaking, two inflectional patterns, one rising and the other falling. On these an infinite variety of changes may be rung and, by means of these changes, the logical and emotional content of a passage is 'pointed.'

This variation of the two patterns may be compared to the variations on a theme in music. The general pattern of the theme is always heard at the same time that the variations upon it are perceived. When an impression of finality is to be given, the voice must often, but by no means always, reproduce a falling inflectional pattern. If the end notes of this pattern are not correctly managed, the voice will be 'dropped,' and inaudibility will result. In order to avoid a dropping of the voice, it must be 'lifted.' This does not mean that it may never go down, but does mean that a falling pattern which slides down from the highest note to the lowest must be rigorously avoided.

> O, how may I
> Call this a lightning?

If Romeo allows this line to sink steadily down to the last stressed syllable which is 'light,' he will, as likely as not, become inaudible. But if the last stressed syllable is 'lifted,' the whole of the final word will be clearly audible even though the voice comes to rest on a note low in pitch. But it is best if the tune of speech is thought of, not as a series of rising and falling patterns, but as if the voice proceeded along a straight line, rising above it or dipping below, as occasion demands. At all costs the deadening effect created by a series of monotonous falls in pitch must be avoided. Inaudibility from this cause is, more often than not, the result of a failure to sustain the thought. It can, and must, be avoided mentally, as well as technically, by carrying the thought right through to the last syllable, and beyond. Do not cease to think until you have ceased to speak.

EXERCISES FOR PROJECTION
Assuming that what has been said about the vocal-technical aspect of projection has been grasped, if not perfected, one should stand in the centre of an imaginary series of concentric circles moving out far beyond one. The area behind the imaginary diameter on which one is standing should now be eliminated from the mind, leaving a semicircular series in front of one. Thus one retains the area most essential to the voice, which should always be imagined as progressing with a forward impetus. In reality, it travels in all directions, but it should always leave the speaker as through an imaginary megaphone.

Exercise 1

Choose a phrase, sentence or speech, and speak with the intention of conveying the logical and emotional content of the lines to the imaginary semicircles, one by one, until the farthest is reached. It is important not consciously to alter the volume of the voice, although this may change, indirectly, in response to the intention to reach the farthest point. At the same time, one should be subconsciously aware of the technical means by which utterance is controlled. All this might have been put more simply, as indeed it has been from time immemorial: 'Always speak for the back row of the pit.' The exercise presents an idea that is the opposite of shouting, which might result from the simpler way of putting it.

Material for developing projection lies to hand in those speeches which are spoken to, and for the especial benefit of, an audience, such as the epilogues to *As You Like It* and *Henry IV*, and a number of the choruses. Use should also be made of Restoration prologues, two of which have been included in this book. In all these the presence of an audience is either implied or stated.

SUMMARY

Such then is the instrument of voice, and such is the way it is managed. It is a highly complex instrument, which must be tuned to perfection, kept at concert pitch, and activated at every performance by the actor's will and feeling. The impact of the actor's mind and soul upon the body, at the moment of performance, sets up a wave of sound which is voice. On this are impressed the movements of speech. In the tone and in the movements reside the feeling and the thought. The movements are felt to take place in the very forefront of the mouth, and not only turn meaningless sound into speech but give definition to the emotions. This complex wave of sound is still further modified by all the infinite variations and combinations of pitch and inflection, volume and stress, pace, timing, and emotional reflexes which, in their turn, are determined and controlled by the rhythm of the play as sensed by the director. The individual contribution of the actor is projected to every part of the auditorium, and so to all the members of the audience, who respond collectively to the intellectual and emotional stimulus which comes to them from the stage.

It is fitting that this book should end with a poem which expresses perfectly the two-way traffic of the theatre – the magic that is in acting itself, the effect of the magic on the audience, and the necessity of the one for the other. Without an audience the actor does not really exist; and for the audience the actor's transient art takes shape each time the auditorium is hushed and darkened.

Never was anything so deserted
As this dim theatre
Now, when in passive grayness the remote
Morning is here,
Daunting the wintry glitter of the pale,
Half-lit chandelier.

Never was anything disenchanted
As this silence!
Gleams of soiled gilding on curved balconies
Empty; immense
Dead crimson curtain, tasselled with its old
And staled pretence.

Nothing is heard but a shuffling and knocking
Of mop and mat,
Where dustily two charwomen exchange
Leisurely chat.
Stretching and settling to voluptuous sleep
Curls a cat.

The voices are gone, the voices
That laughed and cried.
It is as if the whole marvel of the world
Had blankly died,
Exposed, inert as a drowned body left
By the ebb of the tide.

Beautiful as water, beautiful as fire,
The voices came,
Made the eyes to open and the ears to hear,
The hand to lie intent and motionless,
The heart to flame,
The radiance of reality was there,
Splendour and shame.

Slowly an arm dropped, and an empire fell.
We saw, we knew.
A head was lifted, and a soul was freed.
Abysses opened into heaven and hell.
We heard, we drew
Into our thrilled veins courage of the truth
That searched us through.

But the voices are all departed,
The vision dull.
Daylight disconsolately enters
Only to annul.
The vast space is hollow and empty
As a skull.

(Laurence Binyon.)

APPENDIX

VOICE AND SPEECH ROUTINES

The following routines have been provided to give an indication of what matter might be included in a simple, short 'warm up' for the actor. They follow the order and principles laid down by Clifford Turner and will, hopefully, encourage you to compose a logical and effective personal warm up, from the exercises already offered in the various sections of this book.

I have not attempted to deal with all that might be required by individual actors; nor to provide therapeutic material for people with particular problems.

Good voice and speech is a habit and requires regular and consistent practice in order to maintain and develop the technique. It is hoped that these routines might form a basis to begin daily practice.

The routines can be used either by an individual, or by groups, wishing to do some kind of vocal warm up before rehearsal or performance.

MALCOLM MORRISON

DAILY ROUTINE – NUMBER ONE

Relaxation and Posture

1. Stand with your feet slightly apart and slump as you stand. Feel your stomach slacken, chest cave in and your head fall on your chest. Over a slow count of ten feel yourself growing. The rib cage should lift away from the pelvis and the head rise to a poised position on the shoulders. Do this three times slowly.
2. When you are standing erect, raise your shoulders towards your ears, screw up the face.
3. Let the face relax quickly, as if you have taken a mask off, until you feel all the wrinkles gone from the forehead and the muscles of the face feel free of tension.
4. When you have let the face go, let the shoulders drop so that your arms hang easily by your sides. Repeat numbers 2, 3 and 4, in sequence, five times.

5. Check your standing position; make sure your shoulders are straight and your head is well balanced on your shoulders. The stomach should be firm but without tension.

Breathing

1. Place the backs of your hands on your lower ribs and breathe in through the nose and out gently through the mouth, feeling an easy swing of the ribs. Do this twenty times. Do not take a lot of breath, just concentrate on feeling the movement of the ribs.
2. Breathe in on the ribs and gently count out to ten on a whisper. Feel that the whisper is just as strong at the count of nine and ten as it was at the count of one. Do this ten times. Don't let all the breath go at once.
3. Breathe in on the ribs and as you do so raise your arms sideways until they are above your head. There should be a slight sense of reaching for something above you, without tension in the shoulders and throat. Pant gently, like a dog, feeling the movement of the diaphragm. Pant in and out five times, then breathe out smoothly, using the air from the ribs, as you lower your arms to your sides. Repeat this five times.
4. Take a breath in on the ribs followed by one on the diaphragm. Sigh out gently on a whispered *AH* sound using the air from the diaphragm, follow this by a whispered *OO* sound using the air from the ribs. Try to sustain each of the vowels for a count of six. Do this five times.
5. Repeat 4, but intone the vowel sounds making sure that the sound is steady and well supported.

Tone

1. Yawn on an *AH* sound feeling the arching of the soft palate. Do this three times.
2. Yawn on each of the following vowels – *OO AH EE*. Do this three times on each vowel.
3. Intone gently, making the vowels very long – 'Who are you?' and 'Can't you see?' Do each sentence three times and ensure that the tone is rich on each of the words.
4. Keep the lips together and make a number of quick 'm' sounds as if you were laughing. Repeat this several times.
5. Say a long *M* sound, as if you had seen something pleasant. Repeat this five times, getting louder each time.

6. Intone the following sentence gently, sustaining all *M* and *N* sounds:

Make me many, many more.

Pitch

1. Speak the following letting your voice rise in pitch on each word:

                             higher

                        and

                   higher

               climb

           voice

        my

      make

    can

  I

Do this five times, taking a slightly higher starting note each time. Make sure that you are speaking, and not singing, each word.

2. Speak the following letting your voice fall in pitch on each word

  I

    can

      make

        my

          voice

            fall

              lower

                and

                  lower

Again, ensure that you are speaking each word.

Articulation

Speak the following three times each, start slowly and gradually increase your speed. Speak very quietly but form each of the consonant sounds distinctly:

The tip of the tongue, the teeth and the lips.
Look at the windmills whirling in the wind.
I'm pulling a long length of string.

DAILY ROUTINE – NUMBER TWO

Relaxation and Posture

1. Stretch and yawn. Feel the muscles in your body stretching and then releasing as you come to a good standing position, hands hanging loosely by your sides and shoulders straight. Do this three times.
2. Push your shoulders forward and then release them so that they are well placed, above the pelvis, and the arms hang easily by your sides.
3. Lift your shoulders up towards your ears, hold them for a count of three and then let them drop heavily. Do this five times.
4. Drop your head on your chest and let it swing heavily and easily from side to side. Don't push the head. Do this five times to each side, then lift it slowly.

Breathing

1. Place your hands on your lower ribs and breathe in and out gently, feeling an easy swing of the ribs. Do this ten times, to relax and feel that everything is working.
2. Breathing in on the ribs to a count of three, raise the arms to your sides at shoulder height. Breathing out over a slow count of six, lower the arms. Repeat this exercise ten times.
3. Breathe in to a count of three and then count out slowly to six. Do this on a whisper. Do this five times, then increase the count to nine and, finally to twelve.
4. Place one hand on the ribs and the other just below the end of the breast bone, on the stomach. Breathe in to a count of three, feeling the ribs expand; then breathe in for a further count of three, feeling the movement of the diaphragm. Sigh out on an *AH* sound, using the air from the diaphragm, then count out steadily to six using the air from the ribs. Do this ten times.
5. Take a breath on the ribs and one on the diaphragm. Using the air from the diaphragm count out to three loudly, then count out to nine, quietly, using the air from the ribs. Repeat this exercise five times.
6. Breathe in on the ribs and diaphragm. Count out to twelve on the diaphragm followed by a count of twelve on the ribs. Whisper this exercise five times. Then repeat, for a further five times, voiced.

Tone

1. Hum any simple tune you know on a *M* sound. Don't push the voice from the throat, just breathe easily and hum gently.
2. Intone the following, feel your voice move forward on each sound:

EE . . . . . . OO . . . . . . M.   M.   M.

Do this six times.
3. Intone the following:

M. M. M. M. M.   MOO
M. M. M. M. M.   MAH
M. M. M. M. M.   MEE

Ensure that the *EE* sound is as full and rich as the *OO* sound.

Pitch

1. Starting on a high note, think of laughing these sounds:

HOO   HAH   HEE
    HOO   HAH   HEE
        HOO   HAH   HEE

2. Repeat exercise 1, but rise in pitch. Do each exercise five times.
3. Count from 1 to 10 beginning on a low note and getting higher on each number.
4. Begin on a high note at the count of ten and speak each number back to one, getting lower with the voice each time.

Articulation

Repeat the following sentences three times each. Speak them quietly but form each consonant sound distinctly:

Stand to and pipe the Captain aboard.
Hot coffee in a proper copper coffee pot.
I've got a lot of chocolate melting in my pocket.

DAILY ROUTINE – NUMBER THREE

Relaxation and Posture

1. Stretch upwards, then release from the waist. Let the head hang between the arms and allow the hands to brush the floor gently. Slowly uncurl the spine until you are in a standing position. Let the head and shoulders hang down until the very last moment.
2. Stand against a wall and bend your knees, keeping your back against the wall. Gradually rise, feeling that you can keep all of the back gently pressing the wall.
3. Step away from the wall and maintain the feeling of a straight spine, with your head balanced immediately above the shoulders.
4. Let your arms hang loosely by your side and gently punch towards the ground.
5. Drop your head forwards and backwards five times and then bring it slowly to an upright position.

Breathing

1. Begin with the simple rib swing exercise described in exercise 1 of routine number two.
2. Breathe in on the ribs and whisper the following:

One and one are two
     (Breathe again)

Two and two are four
Four and four are eight
     (Breathe again)

Eight and eight are sixteen
Sixteen and sixteen are thirty-two.

3. Repeat number 2 – using voice. Do this three times and then gradually increase the volume as you speak it a fourth and fifth time.
4. Breathe in on the ribs and in on the diaphragm and count to ten on the diaphragm and then ten on the ribs.
5. Breathe in on the ribs and in on the diaphragm. Using the air from the diaphragm count up to ten slowly, gradually increasing the volume as you progress. Once the air from the diaphragm has been used then count back down to one, using the air from the

ribs, getting quieter as you go. The exercise should end with a whispered count of one.

Tone
Intone the following, repeating each pattern three times:

1. No no no no no
2. Nee nee nee nee
3. Moo moo moo moo
4. Mah mah mah mah
5. No moh nee mah
6. Repeat the first five exercises at various pitches.
7. Whisper the following sentence, then intone it and finally speak it:

Many maids milking on a May morning.

Articulation
Repeat the following sentences three times each:

1. Two flew through the window.
2. Try to attend and take the test.
3. Clean the car as quickly as you can.

Repeat the following three times. First whisper it then speak it:

Articulatory agility
Is a desirable ability
Manipulating with dexterity
The tongue, the palate and the lips.

DAILY ROUTINE – NUMBER FOUR

Relaxation and Posture

1. Swing your arms, forwards and backwards. Feel the weight of the hands and imagine it is that weight that is causing the arms to swing. There should be no sense that you are 'working' from the shoulders. Do this ten times to the front and back.
2. Rotate the shoulders towards the back and then swing the arms backwards and forwards three times. As the shoulders drop, the arms should begin swinging. Again, try to avoid the sensation that you are working from the shoulders. All should be easy and heavy. Repeat the sequence ten times.
3. With feet slightly apart (nine inches) gently drop the head from side to side. As you are bringing the head up from the shoulder, feel it balance for a moment, without tension, in the upright position, before you allow it to fall to the opposite side. Do this five times each side.
4. Repeat the exercise described in 3, but let the head fall forward and back instead of from side to side.
5. Check your standing position by placing a finger on the top of your head and lightly stretching towards it. Let the arms hang easily by the sides. Check that the hands are released and are not curled up or the fingers stretched.

Breathing

1. Begin by breathing in on two parts (ribs and diaphragm). The intake of air should be done to a count of three and the expiration of the breath should take a count of five each on diaphragm and ribs. Repeat this ten times.
2. Breathe in on the ribs, then take a very small, easy breath on the diaphragm and say, 'One', then count out to five using the air from the ribs. Be aware that you will need to take very little air on the diaphragm. Repeat this ten times.
3. Repeat exercise 2, increasing the rate at which you do it. Beware of building tension. Do not 'overbreathe'. Only take the minimal amount of air needed for the task. Do this five times.
4. Using the breath from the diaphragm, with the air maintained in the ribs for support, speak the following, gradually getting louder:

My voice is getting very loud.

Repeat this five times. Then, instead of a gradual crescendo, begin by speaking loudly but allow the voice to become quieter. You should finish on a whisper. Beware of overdoing the loudness. The importance of the exercise is in the control over the breath. There should be no sudden jumps in volume. The sound should gradually swell and die away.

Tone

1. Repeat:

   niminy niminy niminy niminy niminy

   several times. Build the appearance of a continuous hum as you say it. Feel that the voice is forward and placed in the mask of the face. Do not force from the throat.
2. Add three N sounds to the above. Keep each one clear and separate from the others. Gradually build the pace as you feel you are able to place the voice easily and instantly:

   n n n niminy   n n n niminy   n n n niminy

   Do this fairly quietly. The important feature of the exercise is the placement of the voice, not the loudness, nor the effort with which you do it.
3. Speak the following sentence a number of times, maintaining the forward placement of the voice and the resonance on the m's and n's:

   Eliminating the naming of many eminently minimal men

Articulation

1. Repeat the following sentences, at speed, first as a whisper, then intoned and finally spoken. Do each sentence five times:

   Jeff met Terry in a friendly set of tennis.

   A record was set when ten men ate twenty lemons.

   Many sensitive men detest the excessive message.

   I met many women when I went to Jenny's event.

DAILY ROUTINE – NUMBER FIVE

Relaxation and Posture

1. Lie on the floor, on your back, and draw your knees up over your chest. Gradually stretch out until the legs are on the floor. Pushing gently, from the heels, feel yourself stretch. Repeat this five times.
2. Gently and easily bring yourself to a sitting position and gently rock from side to side. The legs should be stretched out in front of you.
3. Kneeling forward, seated on your heels, gradually stretch from the waist and torso as you gently push your head towards the ceiling. Do this rhythmically and without excessive effort.
4. Stand up and flop forward from the waist, gradually returning to a standing position, feeling the spine gradually uncurl and the head coming into position last.

Breathing

1. Raise your arms sideways above the head as you breathe in to a count of three and then breathe out to a count of five. Feel the ribs swing out as you breathe in. As you breathe out, make sure the mouth is open and relaxed. There should be barely any sound.
2. Repeat exercise 1 but count out to five on a whisper. Ensure that 'five' is as strong as 'one'; there should be no fading away.
3. Continue exercise 2 but elongate the vowels in each count. Let each word flow smoothly into the other:

    O-o-o-ne two-o-o-o three-ee-ee-ee fou-ou-ou-r fi-i-i-ve

    Repeat this exercise ten times, making sure that the breath flow is slow and consistent in strength.
4. When you have achieved exercise 3 on a whisper, repeat adding voice.
5. Breathe in on the ribs and then pant lightly for a count of ten using only the diaphragm. At the count of 'ten', allow the air retained by the ribs to be expelled on a long sigh of 'Ah'. Do this five times.
6. Speak the alphabet from A to M using breath from the diaphragm, then continue from N to Z, using breath from the ribs. Do this five times on a whisper. Then repeat with voice.

Tone

1. Whisper, intone and then speak the following:

Anon the new moon wanes
and summer nights are gone
Autumn comes mid mild, mild rains
and dark descends ere long

Articulation

1. Repeat the following several times. Gradually increase speed as you do so:

ch ch ch s/	ch ch ch s/	ch ch ch s
l l l v/	l l l v/	l l l v
w w w k/	w w w k/	w w w k

2. Repeat several times:

Will you won't you
Join the chains to each edge
Change the justifying switch

Overdo the movement of the lips. Speak on a whisper first, extending the movements and gaining pace.

INDEX